THE CHANNEL
of
CLARITY
Method

THE PROVEN WAY TO CHANNEL YOUR GUARDIAN ANGEL

Live Your True Life Purpose

Ros Place

GET YOUR FREE BOOK BONUSES

Especially for you, please enjoy your free book bonuses with compliments from myself and Tressarn. Please download your free bonuses as soon as possible to support you to gain deeper insight as you read The Channel of Clarity Method book.

FREE BONUS 1 - GUARDIAN ANGEL WALKTHROUGH

Revealing over-the-shoulder training where Ros and Tressarn walk you through their unique life-purpose strengths. A candid example of a life purpose path with teaching that provides deeper insight into how to find, follow and live your own true life purpose.

FREE BONUS 2 - YOUR LIFE PURPOSE AREAS

One of the most-loved aspects of coaching students is Ros's deeper dive into each of the Life Purpose Strength Areas. In this video training, you'll explore what those life-purpose areas are and how to connect them with your unique life-purpose strengths.

FREE BONUS 3 - CHANNEL OF CLARITY PDF BOOK

Enhance your reading experience with the printable PDF version of this book. See all the colours and enjoy all the self-assessments and life purpose discovery exercises inside the PDF version of the book.

You can access your bonuses with my compliments here:

channelofclarity.com/book-bonus

With love to you and your guardian angel,

Ros & Tressarn xx

To Tressarn for sharing the Channel of Clarity Method and to the friends and guardian angels who use it every day. Thank you.

> "There is no greater agony than hearing an untold story inside you."
> - Maya Angelou

The Channel of Clarity Method

Copyright ©2022. Ros Place. All rights reserved. No part of this book may be reproduced by any mechanical, photographic, or electronic process, or in the form of a phonographic recording; nor may it be stored in a retrieval system, transmitted, or otherwise be copied for public or private use—other than for "fair use" as brief quotations embodied in articles and reviews—without prior written permission of the publisher.

Edited by Linda M. Verde, lindaverdeediting.ca, lindav287@gmail.com

Disclaimer: The author makes no guarantees to the results you'll achieve by reading this book. All life purpose development requires application and hard work. The results and client case studies presented in this book represent results achieved working directly with the author. Your results may vary when undertaking any new life purpose direction or path.

Published by Press of Love   www.pressoflove.com

Contents

Introduction

    How to Read This Book 3

Part 1: How Things Are

    Chapter 1: Who This Book (and Message) is For 11

    Chapter 2: A Day in the Life 29

    Chapter 3: The Three Life Purpose Problems
                 (And How to Solve Them With Your
                 Guardian Angel) 47

    Chapter 4: Your Guardian Angel is the Key 85

    Chapter 5: The #1 Problem with Guardian
                 Angel Connection 101

Part 2: The Channel of Clarity Method

    Chapter 6: The Celestial Formula 109

    Chapter 7: Creating Your Channel of Clarity
                 Step by Step 119

    Chapter 8: How to Have Meaningful and Productive
                 Conversations with Your Guardian Angel 135

Part 3: Getting to Know Your Guardian Angel

    Chapter 9: The First Step for Connecting with
                Your Guardian Angel 149

    Chapter 10: Three Core Elements all Guardian
                 Angels Have in Common 155

    Chapter 11: How to Connect with Your
                 Guardian Angel 163

    Chapter 12: How to Discover Your Unique Life
                 Purpose Strengths 175

    Chapter 13: Building Your Relationship with
                 Your Guardian Angel 219

Conclusion: Starting Your Life Purpose Journey

    What to Do Next? 235

    Book Bonuses 239

    We Can Help You Even More 243

    About the Author 247

Introduction

How to Read This Book

This book exists for two reasons:

Reason #1: To give you the missing piece that is absent from self help books and the reason you're reading them all but not getting anywhere.

Reason #2: So you can live a life that you love every day together with your guardian angel and receive all the guidance, support, and direction you will ever need to find, follow, and live your true purpose in life.

As you'll soon find out, I'm going to be fully transparent, honest, and open with you throughout the pages of this book. My early mentor taught me that if you want people to believe you can help them, help them.

I want to help you.

To do that, I've structured this book as follows:

First, I want you to get an honest picture of where you are today on your life purpose path. That way, I can give you specific guidance and advice, through this book, based on your needs right now. You'll be completing several self-assessments that help you know how best to proceed, based on my 18-plus years of being a guardian angel channel and my mentoring hundreds of clients to find their life purpose path successfully.

After that, I'll share how communication with your guardian angel provides a life purpose path guidance system and, hopefully, show you why communicating with your guardian angel is the answer to your life purpose path struggles.

We'll take a look at what you can expect from your life purpose path and how it is the exact opposite of what many women expect. We'll explore the surprising results of choosing to follow your life purpose path and the types of improvements that your choices create.

Along with the good stuff, we'll take a look at why you might *not* want to communicate with your guardian angel to find your life purpose path, and all the ways people waste time on an emotional roller coaster of hope and disappointment.

Next, I'll share with you **The Celestial Formula** that ensures living your life purpose with your guardian angel is imminent and guaranteed. This is the method I personally use to help my clients succeed in finding their life purpose path. I'm excited to share it with you here.

After that, we'll spend a lot of time focusing on how to have meaningful and productive conversations with your guardian angel that will fit perfectly into the **Channel of Clarity** method. I'll show you how to connect with your guardian angel with a step-by-step process you can easily follow.

Finally, you'll learn about the core life purpose strengths and discover your likely top three unique life purpose strengths and what to do next to live your true purpose in life with your guardian angel.

It might sound like a lot, but really, the entirety of this book can be summed up in the following three points:

> **Point #1:** You have a guardian angel by your side right now, ready to guide you to live your true life purpose.
>
> **Point #2:** When you connect and communicate with your guardian angel you will receive all the life purpose guidance and direction you will ever need.
>
> **Point #3:** The best way to receive life purpose guidance and direction from your guardian angel is through a clear as crystal two-way communication channel.
>
> Tressarn and I call it the **Channel of Clarity.**

The method you're about to discover has radically transformed my life for the better, with benefits far beyond spiritual and personal development. I hope you'll be able to make the connection for yourself as well.

Above all, it is my sincere hope that you learn more than just how to implement **Channel of Clarity**. I've interspersed little bits of advice and lessons I've learned from 18-plus years as a professional Guardian Angel Channel. I was born with the ability to communicate with angels and want, with all my heart, to make the most of my gift and help others to do the same. Yes, this is a spiritual acceleration book, but it's really a book about creating a better life for yourself and those you care about; a life that brings you true joy, spiritual and personal rewards, and a lifetime of peace.

We are in an exciting time of change that I believe will bring in a better world and we will see it within the next generation. So many people are becoming aware of their spiritual selves; they and the children who are coming with the purpose of creating a new world are the ones who will bring it in. It is those who know that there is more to them than the world tells them there is, the seekers of personal freedom and truth, those whose hearts guide them to be the best they can be so they can be their best for the world, they are who will make it happen.

So, it's a great privilege to share what I know with you. I hope it inspires and informs you to have a lifetime of meaningful conversations with your guardian angel, so you can find your life purpose path and live the glorious life you came here for.

Helping women like you to communicate with their guardian angel and to succeed in finding, following and living their true life purpose is exactly what I do, day in and day out.

We're here to help.

To your glorious life purpose success,

Ros and Tressarn xx

Ros Place

Part 1

How Things Are

Chapter 1

Who This Book (and Message) is For

"When we strive to become better than we are, everything around us becomes better too."
– Paulo Coelho

This book exists because of all of the amazing people I've had the good fortune to connect with over my 18 years working as a guardian angel channel. It's for all the women who have had their lives transformed by their guardian angels, after years of 'doing the work' and having experienced frustrating spiritual and personal development.

It's for the women who felt like they are stuck with the life they were living. The women who think that their life is as good as it is going to get and that they should find a way to grin and bear it. For the women who feel they must accept that things are never going to get better.

There's also a personal backstory to this book that I'd like to share with you to show what happens when you resist following your true life purpose path. In 2016, I took a trip alone to Los Angeles and despite not knowing a soul, a chance meeting in a coffee shop led to a series of surprising meetings with high profile people from the music and entertainment industry. My path in Los Angeles eventually led me to be introduced to a gracious billionaire, who invited me to meet him at his spectacular mansion overlooking the sea at Malibu. We spent a wonderful afternoon together where we sat talking with his guardian angel about his life purpose.

Once we talked with his guardian angel for some time, he looked at me and said:

"Ros, what do you want?"

"I don't want anything," I said.

He replied, "You must want something, Ros."

I was without words. It was as though I was being offered the chance to have anything my heart desired.

"I am going to the kitchen to talk with my chef. When I come back, you need to have an answer for me."

He left the room and the clock was ticking. When the gracious billionaire came back, he sat down in his chair, smiled kindly and said, "So, Ros, what do you want?"

I looked him straight in the eyes and I replied, "Can you help me to help children?"

He paused and looked at me for a moment, smiled, and said "Ros, do you like Margaritas?"

I replied, "I love Margaritas."

So he fixed us a Margarita each and we sat on his terrace looking out to the sea in Malibu, talking about being a parent, life in general, and enjoyed a wonderful afternoon together. At the end of the afternoon we swapped phone numbers and he told me to call him and he'd help me.

As I left in my Uber, I knew that the gracious billionaire would help me, but he'd given me a gift that was far more significant and valuable than his offer of help. He helped me to realise that more important than anything to me was to be able to help as many people as possible to connect with their guardian angels. He had filled me with a wonderful realisation that began to glow inside of me like a fantastical light in my heart. Finally, I felt fully focused on my true purpose. I knew I had to connect as many people as possible with their guardian angels, so they could find and follow their life purpose path.

This wonderful realisation was soon replaced with an almost paralysing fear. How could I possibly connect enough people with their guardian angels? Would it be possible for me to connect with any more than a thousand people with their guardian angels? Maybe two thousand people would be possible in my lifetime…

The task felt impossible, I felt insufficient and totally incapable.

So, I gave up.

I gave up channeling guardian angels for two whole years. I was so convinced of the impossibility of my task, that I built an entire other business to help me avoid the inevitable failure that I felt I would be. And whilst this business did well, I was frustrated with a feeling that I wasn't truly being myself. I wasn't authentically, honestly, truly sharing my gift.

I was giving up on my heart's desire to help as many people as possible connect with their guardian angels, and I was giving up on myself. My insistence on turning my back on the angels and my purpose happened before in my life, and each time it led to heartache. I turned my back on the angels for the first time when I was 11. Until age 11, I believed that everyone could see, hear, and talk with angels as I did. It was such an ingrained part of my life that I assumed everyone else did it too. I vividly remember standing in the school playground by the Geography huts and shutting down my entire connection with the angels. So desperate was I to fit in and be like everyone else. It was a traumatic event that marked the beginning of an extremely unhappy and soulless adolescence and early adulthood.

Less than two years after turning my back on the guardian angels, because I didn't feel that I could help enough people to connect with their guardian angels, we lost our family home. We found ourselves homeless with an extremely pared down collection of our belongings stored in a shipping container in East Sussex.

The upheaval of moving our whole lives with our young sons was heartbreaking.

We moved to the north of the country to live a much simpler life and rebuild. In this space and time there was a cracking open in me. I felt completely crushed and humiliated by our circumstances and I was deeply humbled and vulnerable. Being cracked open had happened before in my life. When I gave birth to each of our boys, the angels found a way back into my life. My vulnerability always allowed them to reach me in ways that my stubbornness and willpower closed off.

So, from this place of vulnerability and completely new beginnings, I started again and my guardian angel, Tressarn, told me that he had the solution to our problem. He would teach me how to teach others to channel their guardian angels.

For many years, I'd been asked by clients to show them how I was able to channel their guardian angel, but I couldn't show them the process. I was born with the ability to channel angels and I never learned *how* it was done, so I found it impossible to explain.

I've never been someone who has found it easy to ask for help. I'd never asked Tressarn to show me how it was done. It was at the moment of cracking open and being vulnerable that Tressarn told me it was time for us to teach others how to channel their guardian angels.

So, it was time.

Interestingly, the time coincided with a time in our world where people more than ever want to know how to connect with their guardian angels and discover their true purpose in life. It is time to teach as many people as possible to find their own truth and trust their own path in a way that no one and nothing can take away from them.

With the kind blessing of some wonderful clients, I have some women's success stories to share with you.

Here are four examples from clients* of how **Channel of Clarity** can help you find your own life purpose path:

> **Client Success Story #1: Gina healed her childhood trauma**
>
> Gina first came to me like many of my clients do:
> - Exhausted by failed therapy
> - Trapped in negative thought patterns
> - In a cycle of self doubt and self sabotage
>
> Gina had spent many years and countless dollars on different types of therapy. She put in the work to heal from the trauma of her past and wanted to finally move forwards positively with her life. Gina was motivated to heal from her past and live her true life purpose for herself and her loved ones too. She knew that finding and following her life purpose path with her guardian angel would free her to be a more loving wife, mother, and friend.
>
> Gina was tormented by an inner knowing that she had much to give and enjoy in her life, but she was exhausted by uncontrollable negative thinking. From the very first time we connected with her guardian angel, her guardian angel acknowledged the existence and cause of the negative thinking. Her guardian angel gave her a specific process to improve her negative thought patterns. She also validated her inner knowing — that Gina was here to heal her personal trauma — and once empowered by the process she was given, discovered how she could help others to do the same.
>
> **Many women I have met, live life with suffocating unresolved trauma and constant self criticism and negative thinking that holds them back from finding their life purpose for their whole lifetime.**
>
> Gina began to implement the Channel of Clarity method. She communicated with her guardian angel and received life purpose guidance through her two-way communication channel. Within 60 days, Gina's life had changed, but not in the way either of us expected.

> **Client Success Story #1: Gina healed her childhood trauma**
>
> You see, the process that her guardian angel gave her improved Gina's negative thinking and ceased it entirely! This new way of being made way for some of the most effective and positive communication I have ever witnessed between a client and a guardian angel.
>
> Simply by following the process her guardian angel had given her, and listening to her personal meditation, Gina successfully moved forward with her life purpose path, entirely from the strategies we'll cover in Part 2 of this book.
>
> The best part for Gina is that she wakes every morning full of excitement for her day full of meaning and purpose. She has found new and positive friends who share her interests. Her life is rich, full of fun and things to look forward to.
>
> If this is the kind of thing you bought this book hoping to discover, you'll be most interested in Channel of Clarity Chapter 8 on how to have meaningful and productive conversations with your guardian angel.
>
> It takes effort at the beginning to create clear communication with your guardian angel, but once you have what you need in place, it's effortless to live true life purpose and do so in ways that ensure ever more life enhancing ways.

> **Client Success Story #2: Lisa was liberated from her self doubt**
>
> Lisa's story is an inspiring one for those looking to make a radical shift beyond their previous conditioning.
>
> In the mid-70s, Lisa grew up in a close knit and hardworking, working-class family. Within her family, any talk of having your own dreams was quickly dismissed and ridiculed as lofty ideas. Any suggestion of wanting something more was actively discouraged. She knew her family expectations were for her to study hard, get to college, get the right job and make them proud. She grew up with the belief that her own ideas were worthless and laughable. Lisa bowed to her family's expectations and worked hard to achieve monetary success in the banking sector, but life eventually took her on a different track. After becoming unwell, she faced the prospect of holding down an unfulfilling career with a chronic illness.
>
> Fast forward a few years, and Lisa discovered the method we teach in Channel of Clarity, contacted me to help her, and said, "I want to help people learn how to breakthrough their childhood conditioning by believing in themselves."
>
> Now, let me be transparent here for a second: I knew this was going to be a real challenge.
>
> It is common for people to want to help others to heal from the same issues they have experienced. I wasn't sure, in the beginning, that Lisa had sufficient levels of self confidence to stick with it until it was done. Fortunately, as soon as I connected with her guardian angel, it was confirmed that I was wrong. (Any of mine or my client's doubts are instantly addressed by our guardian angels to remove any question marks.)
>
> As it turns out, Lisa discovered deep reservoirs of self confidence

> **Client Success Story #2: Lisa was liberated from her self doubt**

that enhanced her ability to teach others to become free from their conditioning.

Communicating with her guardian angel helped Lisa to learn specific healing modalities and to build a successful business helping others. She healed herself to live her true life purpose, free from conditioning.

I share Lisa's story to show you what passion and a love for helping others can do with the Channel of Clarity method. I'm so happy for the life purpose business that her guardian angel helped her create, but I'm more excited to report that Lisa is now working full time in her life purpose business and cannot recall experiencing better health.

It's incredible the kind of impact and reach you can have, when you use these methods to help other people and yourself. Sure, it's going to be easier for you if you already have experience helping others, but, if you're willing to work hard and give yourself fully to the task, anything is possible.

> **Client Success Story #3: Maria sees her project through to the end**
>
> Maria came to us the same way Lisa did, with a desire to make a positive difference in her own life and in the lives of others, too.
>
> Maria's desire was very similar with a few exceptions I think are worth noting:
>
> - Maria had a history of starting but not finishing things. She was a self confessed shiny object addict. Maria had a trail of unfinished creative projects and incomplete ideas throughout her life that eroded her self confidence and caused her to doubt her ability to make lasting changes in her life.
>
> - Within the first week of exploring her life purpose path with **Channel of Clarity,** she had a major breakthrough by discovering that she was being stopped in her tracks by *the emotional cycle of change.* She discovered why she didn't finish things in the past.
>
> - Within the first month, she had created almost half of her project and her creative energy was pouring into every area of her life. She even found energy and inspiration to keep a journal full of ideas for future projects.
>
> - Within three months, despite work and family commitments, her first creative project was in final production and was even receiving commercial interest.
>
> This pattern of success, from purpose driven creative idea to successful completion and accomplishment, became Maria's new normal. Before implementing **Channel of Clarity,** Maria struggled to find a reason to keep going with her ideas and was looking for an outlet, reason, or purpose for her creativity. Her skills and talents deserve to be shared and appreciated. For Maria, the methods we

> **Client Success Story #3: Maria sees her project through to the end**
>
> teach in this book were just what she needed to believe in and value herself and her creativity.
>
> For Maria, finding her life purpose path has been a game-changer. She's now working on new creative projects and finding new outlets for sharing her passion and her love for her work.
>
> If you are looking for ways to discover and share your abilities and talents, you'll want to focus on Chapter 12 in this book, where we talk about your unique life purpose strengths.
>
> By finding your life purpose path and expressing your creativity and passion, you'll experience deep fulfillment and you can fill the hole that only true purpose can fill.

Client Success Story#4: Clare the working mum creates family and work harmony

I want to highlight this story to share what some people just won't admit to:

It doesn't always work the first time.

Clare came to me having just made huge changes in her personal and work life. She recently quit her highly successful corporate career due to physical and emotional burnout. Clare's burnout had been a gradual process of mental, physical, and emotional exhaustion after many years of trying to be all things to all people. Excessive and prolonged stress had left her feeling overwhelmed and emotionally, mentally, and physically drained. Perhaps, most upsetting to Clare was that the effects of burnout had spilled into every area of her life — including her closest relationships.

Clare was one of those women who looked like she had it all. The high level career, the husband, children, beautiful home, cars, and exotic vacations. But, all of this came at the expense of her own mental health, a strained relationship with her husband, and a fading connection with her children.

Clare already knew she could have monetary success but she wanted to find a way of living her life that brought harmony and connection into her family and her home.

We were filled with excitement, implementing Channel of Clarity to bring Clare's life purpose path into alignment with both monetary success and relationship harmony. We all had high hopes. Clare was already counting the ways she'd spend her time slowing down to heal and the harmony she'd experience in her life and connection with her family.

Client Success Story#4: Clare the working mum creates family and work harmony

Then reality hit, as it often does when things don't happen precisely as expected. For the first month, Clare felt a crisis of identity and high levels of guilt about not working as she once had. She found it challenging to manage her own time and to feel valuable. Her new open diary made her feel uncomfortable and not productive enough. Since Clare left her position, colleagues were constantly reaching out with ever more enticing offers to come back. A better package, more flexible hours a three-day week... For a good while, she felt as if going back to the life she hated, the life that almost destroyed her and her family, might be her only option.

Sometimes, this happens. Anyone who tells you their method works 100 percent of the time, the first time out, is not telling the truth.

What separates the successful people from the unsuccessful, is their persistence and willingness to keep trying. Wisely, Clare chose persistence. Together with her guardian angel, she gave herself fully to making space to connect and enjoy their relationship. Channel of Clarity gave her the ability to connect and communicate with her guardian angel and create life together. She found that her career taught her the value of working with others as a team. Creating life together with her guardian angel as a team was refreshing, empowering, and exciting. Clare went from feeling totally lost in her new life, to finding true harmony and connection within herself with the love and support of her guardian angel.

Within the first week of finding harmony and connection within herself, she was able to be truly present to her family and her life for the first time ever.

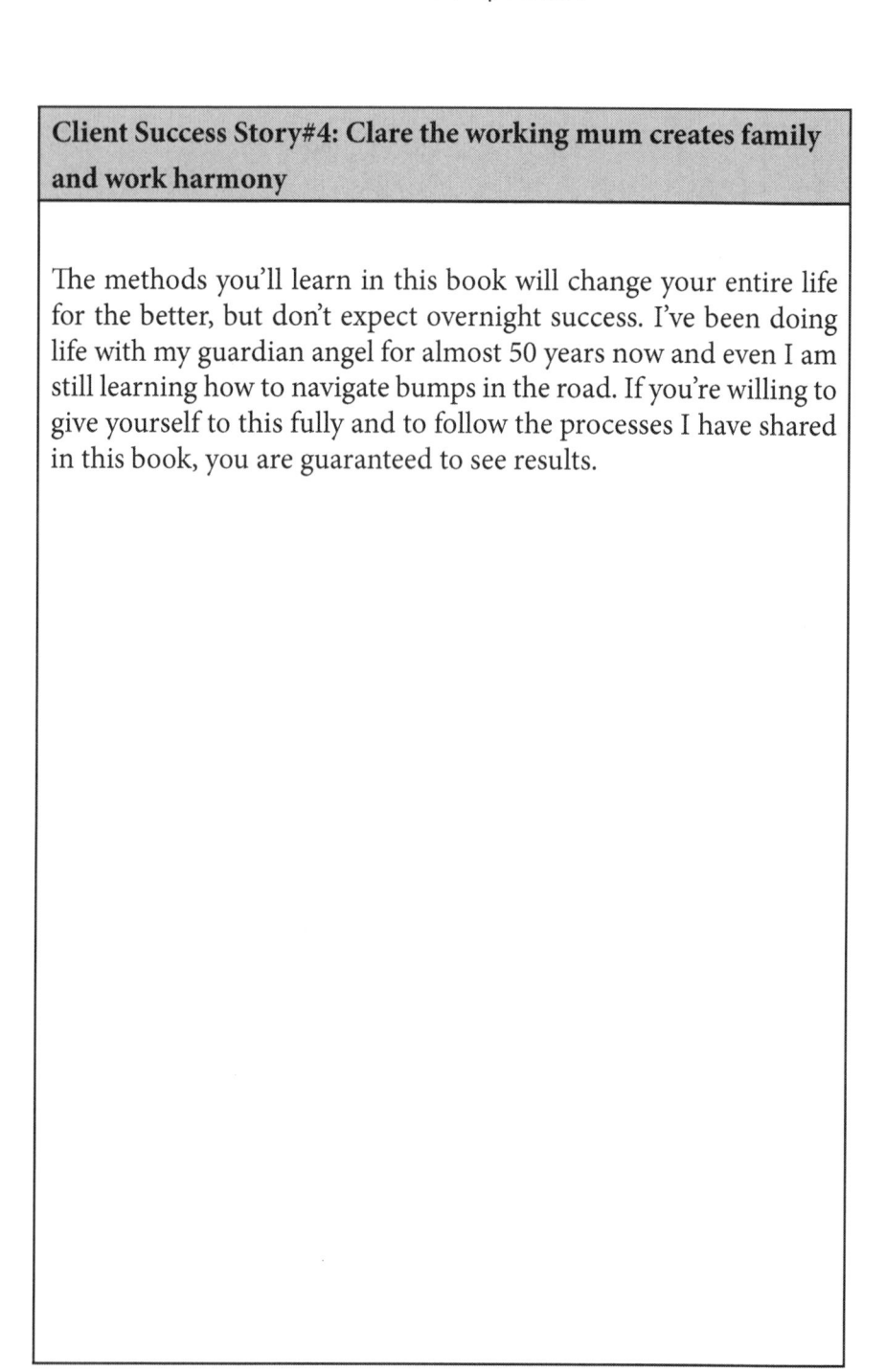

> **Client Success Story#4: Clare the working mum creates family and work harmony**
>
> The methods you'll learn in this book will change your entire life for the better, but don't expect overnight success. I've been doing life with my guardian angel for almost 50 years now and even I am still learning how to navigate bumps in the road. If you're willing to give yourself to this fully and to follow the processes I have shared in this book, you are guaranteed to see results.

As you can see, there are many different ways that **Channel of Clarity** can improve your life for the better. Later, I'll share with you the exact method I'm using to make that happen, but for now, consider this:

Connecting with your Guardian Angel to find and follow your life purpose path brings your highest and most positive version of success. Nothing is sacrificed.

What makes your life purpose path personally enriching and enjoyable also makes it personally fulfilling and successful.

You don't need to be a spiritual master (or even to have considered yourself spiritual for that matter). You don't need to be someone who has always known what they want in life. Many of the most interesting women I have worked with, have begun from a place of having either forgotten or never previously considered what makes them happy. You don't need to be someone who has done this kind of thing before (many of my clients are from science based backgrounds, academic, the corporate world, legal professions, or medical doctors.) I enjoy connecting with an exciting variety of women from all walks of life, all wanting to find their life purpose path, thanks to the method I am sharing with you here.

If you struggle to find your true purpose in life with peace in your mind, body, and soul and you seek the true success of deep personal fulfillment, I can help you to achieve measurable and life changing results.

It is within your power to find and follow your life purpose path, so, instead of guessing and hoping you'll find the way, you'll know your precise direction. A distinct life purpose path instead of wandering through life constantly looking for signs to guide you.

In the pages of this book, I outline, as best I can, the important steps that help you to connect with your guardian angel, so you can live your true purpose in life with your own **Channel of Clarity.**

It's possible that your guardian angel could be the life purpose guide you've been looking for. The only way to find out for sure is to read every letter of this book. It should take you less than a few hours to finish, but can unlock the life purpose guidance and direction that you've been missing all along.

So, if you're ready to take my hand and allow me to show you, here's your chance to change the nature of your life purpose path, let's go!

Ros Place

Chapter 2

A Day in the Life

"Your life does not get better by chance, it gets better by change."
– Jim Rohn

What I want you to take away most from this book is that communicating with your guardian angel is the fastest, easiest, most enjoyable, and most fast-tracked way to find, follow, and live your true purpose in life.

Most people when asked what they want in life answer that they just want to be happy. Many women I have worked with have been searching for something elusive for many years. Purely and simply, they want to experience happiness and peace in their lives, and to find contentment.

Clients often talk about how they are searching for answers and direction, feeling that they are at the mercy of everything that is happening around them. They describe feeling overwhelmed by all the noise and stress of life, and simply wanting to find peace.

From the moment of first connection with their guardian angel, clients describe feeling that a light inside of them has been switched on and it is showing them the way forward.

The women I work with describe something so simple yet profound — they no longer feel lonely. They no longer feel that they're missing something. They feel that the hole inside of them that has been empty for so long, now feels full. They explain that they feel connected to themselves in ways which have been absent for their entire lives. Women describe living every day deeply aware that they are on the right path and know that they are moving in the right direction.

We've all heard stories of those who suffered illness and how their recovery caused them to view their entire life in a completely different way. They feel that they've been given a second chance to truly live life. Some women describe the experience of implementing the Channel of Clarity method as comparable to having been given a second chance at life.

Physical changes are reported, such as seeing yourself in the mirror and noticing you look younger, more youthful, lighter. Women say they feel like their younger self, yet living in a more mature and experienced body and life. Something new and rejuvenated radiates from inside.

Women reveal that their relationships are working. They feel connected with the people that they care about. They feel a deep sense of love and connection with others and heal relationships that have been stressful or fraught with difficulties in the past.

A feeling of being fully content in the present is described -- and the realisation that they want for nothing. They are able to see the beauty in life. Small things make them happy and they feel as though their eyes are seeing their life truly for the very first time.

Clients regularly reach out to report what others may see as suddenly becoming lucky and how rapid solutions and positive outcomes arrive thick and fast in all areas of their life.

I often receive communication from clients to tell me that they have been promoted, got a pay raise, found love, healed a relationship, shed unwanted weight or that some other opportunity that they have been seeking for some time suddenly appears.

All of these results and countless more are possible when you know your life purpose — and you choose to live it.

You are about to learn a method that comes from one of my big life lessons. In 2019, when we lost our home and the life we had worked so hard to create, it was crushing and painful. I had turned my back on my life purpose path and the result was disastrous.

This was not a case of trying to *find* my life purpose path — I *knew* it; yet, I still chose not to follow that path. When you meet my guardian angel, Tressarn, later in this book, you will see how clear my life purpose is.

In the rubble from the collapse of our life, and from within my crushing feelings of humiliation, Tressarn finally reached me in a way that was impossible to ignore. I realised what I had done and I felt ridiculous — the humiliation became humility. Breaking through my vulnerability, he showed me how we could focus on my life purpose path *together* in ways that were impossible for me to do by myself.

There is a saying that knowledge is power. I disagree. Knowledge, in itself, is not power. Knowledge *applied* is power. Knowing my life purpose path was only the first step. The moment I chose, once again, to live my life purpose together with Tressarn, everything changed.

Tressarn and I began having *meaningful* and productive conversations. He taught me how to formulate and ask the right kind of questions, so he could provide clear and direct answers. Together, we created a *conversation* that guided me along my life purpose path.

Today, just three short and very happy years on, despite living through homelessness, two business collapses, and unprecedented global disruption, as a family we are fulfilled and content. My husband Eddie, has retired from a career he had outgrown in IT, to follow his own true life purpose path. We are working towards our family dream of a small farm with fertile land, fruit trees, some goats, a dog for my younger son and a small woodland we can take care of for birds and wildlife.

Today and every day, we are fulfilled and content with what we have, and excited about what is yet to come. I am living my life purpose path, and my husband and both our boys are living theirs, together with our guardian angels.

I am sharing this with you so you can see that, although I made big mistakes, it is never too late to find and focus on your life purpose path. Just knowing your path is not enough; you must act to truly derive its benefits.

Tressarn and I are working together to help as many people as possible to communicate with their guardian angels, so they can find, follow and live their life purpose path. Here's the story of how I came to write this book for you.

Tressarn and I spent many, many hours communicating during the past two years. He showed me how to create what he calls a Channel of Clarity to receive, from your guardian angel, clear answers and all the life purpose guidance you will ever need. This channel of clarity is effective from a woman's very first ripple of spiritual awareness. It requires no previous spiritual experience or study and works equally for those who have been on their spiritual path for many years and those who are just taking their first steps.

After many hours of development with Tressarn, I reached out to a small number of clients and asked them if they would like me to teach them how to channel their guardian angel so they could find and follow their true life purpose. These were clients who had experienced me channeling their guardian angel for them in the past. They had seen, already, that channeled communication with their guardian angel provides clear answers and accurate life purpose guidance.

What was different this time was that I was offering to teach my clients how to do for themselves what I had done for them. Tressarn and I were still developing the process and we were hoping to get constructive feedback from the clients' experimentation. I explained that Tressarn would guide their guardian angels, while I guided them. Everyone I reached out to said yes.

Let me share Jessica's story with you so you can see how learning to channel her guardian angel helped her to find and follow her life purpose path.

Jessica 46

Jessica is married with two children. Outwardly, she's a very successful executive working for a large international corporation. Jessica has worked hard to make progress through her company, while raising a family, and has made sacrifices to progress in her career. She seems to be a woman who has life nailed. Inwardly, that was not the case. Jessica reached out to me because she was struggling to cope with daily life.

At night, Jessica often thought about ways to escape the life she had created for herself. She'd lie there, wrestling with her thoughts, desperately wanting her mind to become calm — to just quiet, so she could get some sleep. Nothing was helping. Trying to force herself not to think just seemed to make more thoughts burst into her mind even louder than before. She told herself that worrying was pointless, but suddenly there was a stream of new things to worry about. She tried fluffing up her pillow, going for another pee, turning onto her back, turning onto her side, but just as she felt herself drift off, she'd jolt awake with another thought.

As the night wore on, her strength drained away. Feeling fragile and broken from fatigue, she eventually fell asleep. When her alarm went off in the morning, she awoke facing another day of trying to make everything work, feeling completely exhausted and miserable. Stress and anxiety caused a sickening knot in her stomach.

She disliked the life she had created. **The life she wanted so much in her late 20s was now running her into the ground.** Life was frantic. Work was expecting more of her than ever before, and her family unit was fracturing. It was a nightmare.

Since she turned 40, she realised that, she disliked the life she had created and it was becoming increasingly impossible to hold things together. Every day, somehow she had to drag energy and motivation up from her very depths. She was frightened that she would soon run out of her inner resources completely.

In the past 10 years, Jessica put on almost 30 pounds, she suffered panic attacks, and her marriage was teetering on the edge of divorce. She felt completely trapped and unable to escape the life she created but no longer wanted.

Our First Important Lesson

Our lives are a result of how they are designed, whether that design takes place on purpose — like Jessica in her 20s — or by accident — merely a reaction to events or without direction or guidance.

The life you are living today is the life you have created and experiencing that life engenders emotions. The hours you work, the work you do, the duties you must perform, and endless obligations to everyone else can leave you feeling you never have enough time, so, to compensate, you keep spreading yourself thinner and thinner. Instead of alleviating the situation, you end up feeling that no one is happy at work or at home, including you. These are possible outcomes of the life you have created.

Whether your life was consciously or accidentally created, makes no difference to your day-to-day life. Without changing your life vision, it can only keep giving you more of the same.

You see, Jessica made the mistake many driven and capable women make. She relied on the woman she was in her early 30s to keep all the plates spinning, even though, over time, she took on more responsibility at work and at home, thinking that by working harder or longer or smarter, life would improve. Yet, she was not replenishing herself to give her more inner resources to cope with the added work and responsibilities. Consequently, her mood fluctuated wildly, based on her ability to complete her endless list of tasks and absorb the stress of her situation. In her mind, her mental and emotional health were tied to her own mind's critical assessment of how well or how much she got done.

From the outside looking in, she was living the charmed life of a successful woman who had it all. She was clearing good money every month and could choose how she spent it. She had the dream house, the husband, the kids, the vacations, the fancy car, and the money. What she didn't have was peace.

To complicate things, she soon became addicted to the struggle. **The stress became normal. The exhaustion became normal. The forgetfulness, caused by her full-to-bursting brain, was laughed off as her age.** The empty feeling of neither being present at work or at home was just the way things were.

Like all addicts, it took hitting rock bottom before she woke up and made a change. I'll spare you the details of Jessica's rock bottom; just know this: the path of pushing on regardless and working harder and harder to keep all the plates spinning is not a rewarding path. Instead, it leads to pain, sickness, burnout, depression, and failed relationships along its way.

Thankfully, Jessica's rock bottom came quickly before the damage was irrevocable. Fortunately, she found the **Channel of Clarity** method before the strain on her marriage was irreparable. She woke up before her kids grew up with a distant and depressed mother. She was able to save her sanity, reduce her stress levels, and return to peak physical health, all due to the one simple change I'll be teaching you about in these pages, specifically, because she changed how she lives her life purpose through her daily life.

There were two particular improvements she saw as soon as she implemented the strategy in this book:

1. Jessica's thoughts became calmer and clearer almost instantly. She felt happier and more content. She had the deepest sleeps she'd had in months and she felt younger and lighter.

2. As a result of her calmer, clearer thinking, she no longer suffered from the exhaustion induced from anxiety, stress, and deep unhappiness. She shed the unwanted weight. She felt a genuine peace, the kind of contentment and happiness that gets into your bones and allows you to invite and embrace the very best of life.

What I'm really going to be teaching you in the pages of this book is how to create a relationship with your guardian angel that provides you with the peace and contentment to live your very best life today, as well as change the very nature of your future.

> ***It matters that life lives through you***
> ***Contentment is life living through you***
> ***-Hokusai Says***

You'll find, once you finish this book and put it into action, that channeled conversations with your guardian angel will lead you to find your life purpose path, and your entire life will improve with significantly less effort than it takes to keep feeding your existing unhappiness.

My goal is to improve your thoughts and feelings *and* to improve the quality of every area of your daily life so you can feel the rejuvenating flow of your true purpose running through your veins.

If you are a woman feeling the first ripples of spiritual awareness and feeling a yearning for satisfaction of a deeper, more spiritual need, this method has specific and unique benefits for you. It requires no chanting, no sitting cross-legged, nor a need for any particular beliefs. There are simple yet powerful steps you can incorporate into your daily life to break the cycle of anxiety, stress, unhappiness, and exhaustion.

You have the advantage of a unique life purpose and the opportunity to make a real and special contribution to the world, whether you realise it or not. I'll be teaching you an approach to finding and following your life purpose path, which is perfectly suited for a woman who knows there is more to her than the life she is currently living.

You may say, "Well, I'm just me. I'm not sure I have anything special or unique to contribute to the world."

By the end of this book, you'll see that precisely by being the you that you truly came here to be, you can positively impact the lives of everyone you love and care about, and I'll teach you how you can live a life you truly love.

It is my sincere hope that by learning the **Channel of Clarity** method, you will be able to live your true purpose. In return, you will enjoy every imaginable abundant opportunity for what is best in life, especially during these difficult times. By following the methods in this book, you'll see that everywhere, from your working environment to your most precious relationships, you are a woman who lives a life of tremendous value and authenticity and who inspires others to do the same.

Of course, above all else, it is also my hope that by taking the time to read this short book, you will see a path forward — a path of genuine peace and deep happiness, with the energy to embrace the life you came here to live.

So, dear reader, this book is for those of you women who, from the first ripple of spiritual awareness, want to satisfy the yearning for something deeper and to find, follow, and live your true purpose in life, rather than struggling through a life that is running you into the ground.

Key Chapter Takeaways

- Our lives are a result of how they are designed, whether that design takes place on purpose or by accident. The hours you work, the work you do, the duties you must perform, and endless obligations to everyone else can leave you feeling you never have enough time and no one is happy.

- It is possible to become addicted to struggle. The stress becomes normal. The exhaustion becomes normal. The forgetfulness, caused by a full-to-bursting brain is laughed off as your age. The empty feeling of neither being present at work or at home can be dismissed as *just the way things are*.

- You have the advantage of a unique life purpose and the opportunity to make a real and special contribution to the world. You can positively impact the lives of everyone you love and care about by living a life you truly love.

Life Purpose Check-in Exercise

Self Assessment

Before we proceed with the rest of the book, let's first check in with where you're at right now in your life. Below, rate yourself on a scale from 1 — 10 of how accurate the statements are—1 means "not accurate at all," and 10 means "most accurate." Once you've rated yourself for each statement, total up your scores, then use the Answer Key to determine your next steps.

Success Check-In Statement	Self-Rating
I do what I love to do every day.	
I know what I love to do.	
My work does not feel like work. Even without financial constraint I'd do the same as I do now.	
I am happy in my life and rarely question if it could be better.	
I forgive myself easily.	
I have several exciting possible opportunities I am looking forward to in the next 12 months.	
I have healed and I am at peace from challenging times from my past.	
I feel valued and appreciated in my life.	
I feel at peace in my life and rarely dream of an escape route.	
I wake up feeling inspired and excited for my day.	
My Score	

What Your Score Really Means

Score: 0 — 25
The Fundamentals Are Missing

The bad news is that your life is missing core, fundamental elements required for long-term happiness. You probably already know and feel this every day. No surprise there.

However, the good news is that all of that can be fixed, and even better, it means you get to experience your true purpose in life from the ground up.

Read this book with an open mind. Consider how implementing **Channel of Clarity** from the ground up could radically improve your life for the better. It won't take much for you to experience an improvement as different as night and day.

Read this book from beginning to end for results from the ground up

.

Score: 26 — 78
A Simple Change of Focus Makes Life Much Easier

If your score landed you here, it means your current approach to life is the thing holding you back from finding your true life purpose.

You likely rely on unsustainable expectations of yourself and unrealistic measures of your energy levels, paired with responsibilities and duties that have you teetering on the edge of overwhelm. You're working way too hard, doing far too much and feeling like there is no way out.

Understanding the life purpose blocks that are holding you back from finding your life purpose path allows you to, for the first time, become free to live your true purpose in life.

Chapter 3 is where you'll discover the universal deep issues that impact women and may be preventing you from living your true purpose in life.

Score: 79+
You're Ready To Live Your Complete Life Purpose

You've got good levels of satisfaction in your life already, you know what you enjoy doing and you make time to do it. All you need is to get clear on the pin point specifics of your unique life purpose and your unique strengths. You have an opportunity to make a real and special contribution to the world. You can positively impact the lives of everyone you love and care about by knowing your life purpose path.

For you, the biggest hurdle to overcome is getting the best life purpose guidance so you can ensure you're living your complete purpose in life. That's where **Channel of Clarity** comes in. You'll receive all the answers, direction, and life purpose guidance you will ever need through a crystal clear two-way communication channel.

Read through Chapter 6 and you'll learn all you need to know to get all the life purpose guidance you'll ever need, then, simply implement the system as shown in this book and you'll be well on your way.

Ros Place

Chapter 3

The Three Life Purpose Problems (And How to Solve Them With Your Guardian Angel)

"The most influential person you will ever meet in your life is You."
-Tressarn

I have helped women from all walks of life find their true purpose path. My clients include CEOs, executives, entrepreneurs and business owners, record producers and international recording artists, lawyers, intensive care unit doctors, and many other professionals.

Working with clients for more than 18 years, individually mentoring or group coaching, I have encountered repeated blocks, which, in their consistency, shine a light on the deeper universal issues that impact us all when seeking our life purpose.

All that is to say, after 18 years of working with clients, many of whom are considered to be at the pinnacle of success, I've learned some things that I want to share with you. Women from all walks of life struggle to experience their true life purpose. From them, I have identified three universal purpose blocks. I want to share these with you for two reasons:

1. so you can learn from them and avoid making the same mistakes yourself; and,

2. to show you exactly why I see how conversations with your guardian angel can help you find your true life purpose path.

Life Purpose Block 1. Fear and Self-doubt

Once I helped a successful veterinary physician. I was helping her fulfill her purpose to write a really meaningful and powerful book. Working with her gave me incredible insight into how someone so smart, so educated, so successful, and such an authority in her field, could still harbour such disabling self-doubt.

She knew exactly what she wanted to write about and had written papers throughout her entire professional life as a vet. Her book was about an issue she witnessed every day in her practice. This was something she cared deeply about and knew could help thousands, perhaps even millions, of animals.

She would email to tell me she was walking and dictating her book. She told me that she reorganized her office space to be more comfortable and welcoming. She reported that she'd had another revelation about what to include in the book. She was doing all of the *preparations* to write her book, yet she was still stuck with a book in her heart and mind that was not getting written.

Does this describe your current experience with getting done the things you want to get done? You spend time getting ready, researching, planning, getting excited about it and then you get stuck, and it doesn't happen.

It's because the more you doubt yourself, the more fearful, self-critical, and less productive you become. **Self-doubt distracts you from making progress and it eats your dreams.**

You see, my client's book could be such a catalyst for good — her daily life and professional career could flourish and improve through her book. But her self-doubt meant that she felt incapable, frustrated, and guilty. These feelings were impacting all parts of her life.

Even the best of us can fall prey to fear and self-doubt at some point in our lives. I know that my progress in life was stalled because of self-doubt and fear. It's part of the human condition and many of us try to convince ourselves that it is a way of keeping ourselves safe in an often-confusing world.

Self-doubt causes us to believe that we are not good enough; that whatever we do, we will never be good enough. Self-doubt undermines our efforts so we avoid the possibility of an even bigger failure. It can be totally immobilising and cause us to do nothing and miss out on incredible opportunities in our lives. Some people fear failure so much that they choose not to try at all.

Fear of failure is a widely recognised issue as far back as Ancient Greece, from which it gets its name – atychiphobia. *"Atychiphobia is an intense fear of failure. It may cause you to put off or avoid any activity or scenario that has the potential for an unsuccessful outcome."*

The combination of fear and self-doubt is the primary purpose block, and it holds women back from releasing their true potential. In a world that values conspicuous wealth-based success, striking out for something you truly believe in, but is not valued by the same measures, can trigger all kinds of self-doubt.

Maybe I'll write another book about how much more enjoyable developing self-belief is, and how it's not enough for people to tell you, "just believe in yourself," or worse, the advice to "fake it 'til you make it." For the sake of this book, here is an important takeaway: **Self-doubt will eat your dreams.**

If you've been stuck in self-doubt yourself, you might already recognise the block that my client was facing. Self-doubt creates fear, and fear prevents you from making progress.

The cost of women's self-doubt is beyond measure. Think of all the ideas unshared, businesses not started, and talents unused. Many women find that self-doubt surfaces most intensely around their deepest hopes and dreams. They can feel panic and overwhelming self-doubt when they are moving towards doing something they love to do. Because we cherish our dreams and hopes, the potential loss or denial of them makes us feel vulnerable.

It is important to recognise that if you have a propensity to think about something you would love to do, then spend time getting ready, research, plan, and get excited, only to get stuck. If you are immobilized by your self-doubt, stuck in your head, trying to work out everything in your mind before you move forward, and, all the while, your fear is telling you all the reasons you are likely to fail, the thing you would love to do doesn't happen.

Put another way, to find your life purpose path, you need to do more of the things you love to do more often and to a greater degree. To follow your life purpose path, what you need is *you*, you with all your strengths, accepting that you are far more than your fears and self-doubt tell you that you are.

Try to remember that you are not your fears. Instead of hiding behind your fears, you can be a woman who is curious and passionate about who she really is. Once you stop fearing you might not measure up to perceived standards, you will discover your greatest champion — you.

If you want to find your life purpose path, this is what you need:

1) a knowledge and understanding of your unique strengths that remove self-doubt;

2) a clear awareness of your life purpose that guides your direction and path; and

3) a way to connect the two.

   With the approach above, time and time again women from every walk of life I have encountered, find their true purpose. Here are a few areas of life in which my clients have found their life purpose by following the above three simple steps:

   - making a contribution to their community
   - contributing time or skill to a cause
   - prioritising home and family

- launching a business
- enriching a team
- finding career success
- living your true self authentically
- enjoying creative expression
- inspiring others
- pursuing a craft or fine art
- coaching a local team
- writing a book
- achieving life harmony
- protecting the environment
- raising successful children
- living with joy and passion
- leaving a legacy
- creating meaningful connections
- helping children
- teaching and sharing wisdom
- empowering others
- helping animals
- prioritising health and wellbeing
- embracing spirituality

- living a happy and ethical life
- reaching your highest and fullest potential
- bringing joy to others
- help those in need ... and more.

No two people have the exact same life purpose — even if they value the same things.

After reading this book, I hope you are left with the desire to conquer any self-doubt you might have, so you can find the fulfilment and joy of your true purpose in life.

For now, take a moment to check in with yourself.

Life Purpose Check-in Exercise

Self Assessment

Before we proceed with the rest of the book, let's first check in with where you're at with self doubt right now.

Below, rate yourself on a scale from 1 — 10 on how accurate the statements are —1 means "not accurate at all," and 10 means "most accurate."

Once you've rated yourself for each statement, total up your scores and then use the Answer Key to determine your next steps.

Self-Doubt Check-in	Self Rating
I am perfect exactly as I am.	
I know what I am capable of.	
I love myself.	
I am here to make a valuable contribution.	
I trust myself.	
I deserve good things.	
I am not held back by fear.	
I take the initiative and make good decisions.	
I learn from my past and shape my future.	
I don't settle for less than I deserve.	
My Score	

What Your Score Really Means

> **Score: 10 — 32**
> **Self-Doubt Is Holding You Back**

You feel exhausted by overthinking, and doubt your ability to ever find your purpose in life. You've had your hopes dashed in the past and this is an effort to try one more thing before you go back to life as normal.

Even if you aren't there right now, if you keep on this path of letting self doubt dictate your life, eventually you'll hit rock bottom. You are on the path to self-destruction as we speak.

Look, I get it. Been there. Done that. Got the t-shirt.

More than anything, what will work best is to choose to stop doubting yourself; to stick with one thing *until* it works, not *if* it works; to choose to tolerate self-doubt no longer; to realise that self doubt ruins your ability to be yourself. In other words, you can stop letting self-doubt keep you from living the life you came to live.

My hope is that the pages of this book show you how you can replace your self-doubt with a proven system for finding and following your life purpose path. Commit to doing it *until*, not *if*, and you'll be well on your way.

Score: 33 — 68
Self-Doubt is Suppressed

You've likely developed an incredible ability to make your life work while struggling with self-doubt. Your self-doubt needs to be pushed down and squashed on an almost constant basis to keep it in check. I call it *self-doubt suppression at all costs*, and it's common, amongst the women that I work with, at the beginning of our work together. If that's you, kudos for creating your life thus far despite this daily battle with self-doubt.

I get it. I have been there.

You're still holding on to limiting levels of self-doubt and the only reason you aren't living your life purpose is that there is still more letting go to do. If you don't change something soon, eventually you'll be dragged away from your true purpose completely.

Relying on one system that removes self-doubt about what you are good at with a strength based approach to life purpose, gives you all you need to validate yourself and your abilities.

Channel of Clarity could be that one system that helps you get there. You may not like what you read today; yet, releasing your limiting levels of self-belief is necessary to live your true purpose in life.

Score: 69+
Time To Get More Help

You are a determined woman and you don't allow self-doubt or fear dictate your choices or direction in life. As a result, you've carved out a life built on good levels of self-esteem.

Your confidence in yourself has provided the momentum to craft your life so far, but now you're ready for more.

If you are reading this book, it is because you want to know your deeper purpose in life. You wonder "Is this it?" about your life. You want to explore that recurring sense that something's missing and get clear on exactly what it is. You want to know how to live your true and complete purpose in life.

It's time for you to get help. The thing holding you back is simply the right strategy to find and follow your true purpose in life.

This book shows you my strategy so you can determine if it is the right one to help you to get the crystal clear guidance and direction you need to take you all the way to living your true purpose in life.

Once you finish this book, you may want to find someone you can trust to put what you have learned into practice and to continue your skill of determination until you are living your true and complete purpose every day of your life.

Life Purpose Block 2. What Others Think

In 2016, I realised I was a people pleaser, trying to be what other people wanted me to be. It dawned on me that I wanted, very much, to be accepted and liked and just to fit in. I wasn't consciously aware of it until then, but there was always a part of me that wanted to please others in order to avoid reactions I feared or would be unpleasant.

In early summer that year, I was at a speaking event in Miami. I remember the sound of my high heels echoing on the marble floor as I walked towards the elevator where I was heading with the producer of the event. An unpleasant feeling crept over me — a physical feeling of intense fear. My mouth was dry, my heart racing, I was sweating, and starting to feel quite sick.

I pressed the button to call the elevator to take me to the floor where I would be speaking and, while we were waiting, I whipped my head towards the producer standing with me and quickly asked, "How shall I be? "

I will never forget the look on her face. She was quiet for a moment, maybe wondering if she needed to talk me down off the ledge, then said, "Be yourself."

That was not the answer I was looking for.

Throughout my life I have changed myself to fit into what I thought other people wanted me to be. When I was in my 20s, I remember a close friend being upset with me because I hadn't been attentive enough; I'd been busy and not called or been out for drinks with her for a while. She told me she missed me and felt like our friendship was drifting away. Immediately, I felt bad and tried to figure out how I could give her what she wanted. I didn't even stop to consider whether or not her demands were reasonable or if what she said was true! I didn't ask myself how attentive I actually had been, or whether her need for a lot of attention was from her own insecurities. My only thought was: How can I please her? How can I get her to stop being upset with me? I was spinning in my head, urgently trying to find ways to be a better friend by her definition, when I hadn't figured out what the problem or its cause was!

On the outside, however, I appeared to be a highly confident woman who took everything in her stride. When I was in my late 30s, I regularly traveled to LA for business. I traveled alone and, in the beginning, knew no one. I had several potentially life changing business meetings, but my main concern was how much do they like me? I didn't ask myself how much I liked them, or if I wanted to work with them, my main concern was how much they liked me.

Looking back, I see that I didn't show up knowing my value or what I could bring to the working relationship. My focus was on pleasing them. I tried to figure out what they were looking for, then morphed into that Ros, without even realising the changes I was making in myself. If I said something they seemed to disagree with, I would immediately change my opinion. If they pitched this idea or that project, I'd find myself thinking this was a fantastic opportunity. I didn't realise I was trying to please them, it just happened.

I could share many more examples of people pleasing in my life. It was a pattern that was constantly being activated. I had a really hard time saying no or setting boundaries. I would go to great lengths to avoid conflict and deeply desired other people's approval. Perhaps, more importantly, I feared other people's disapproval. If someone asked me for something I had a hard time not giving it to them.

As humans, a part of us wants to know we are appreciated and valued and it is important to honour this part of who we are. However, it is not the part that should be running your life. For our overall well-being, it is healthy to detach from both the dependency on others' praise and the fear of their disapproval.

Part of it is cultural. One of my clients was raised in a family where standing out — even for positive reasons — was met with disapproval. She learned from the time she was a little girl that she should keep herself small and not get noticed. She worked at a large corporation and came to me for help when she recognised she was being passed over for promotions. Through our work together, she realised that she had been holding herself back because she was afraid of being too successful and receiving too much praise.

So many women never talk about their accomplishments and prevent their own success in order to avoid being the target of praise. Something I see regularly in clients is, perhaps, a more hidden way of women getting trapped in the praise and criticism cycle — self-sabotage. The praise and criticism cycle is something many women learn as young girls when they receive praise for being a *good* girl, which means conforming to cultural ideas of how a good girl should act, how they should look, and even how they should think. Being a good girl was rewarded with high levels of approval and was often a condition of receiving love from parents.

The implicit message young girls receive from this is "Be the way I want you to be — that's all that matters. Be nice. Be likable. Be quiet. Be considerate of others. Above all, don't rock the boat. And, if you ever dare to show me anger, independence, or assertion, I will withdraw my love and attention." I got that message loud and clear. Such messages of conditional acceptance program our future relationship dynamics. Being a good girl becomes our default setting. It shapes all of our relationships, directs our careers, and guides every choice we make in our lives.

It's literally impossible to please everyone. No matter what you choose to do in your life, someone will not be pleased. Someone is going to have an opinion about which path you follow or which direction you choose. You may be judged on what you do for your career, what you did for your education, what you said in the meeting, where you suggested to go for lunch, what time you leave your desk, who your friends are, the clothes you wear, the places you spend your time, how much money you make, where you take your vacation, and anything else beyond.

Think of how different all of the people are that you have in your life today. They all have unique viewpoints and ideas of what they believe is the best way to live. You may be able to please more than one, but how can you expect to please them all when they may well have contradictory views? Thinking through this is important and a valuable exercise.

For example, consider the many ideas around the globe about what a woman's role is in the world. There was a time when that was defined by your family or community. Now, women are bombarded regularly through global marketing and social media connections and pressures, all trying to get us to conform to a certain way of being, telling us that by doing so we will please others and find success.

It's tempting to think that we only have a few people to please. You know, only your boss, your partner, maybe your parents, so you think you can manage to keep up the facade. But don't be fooled. The good girl's desire to please runs deep and women find themselves in increasingly impossible situations.

I see a tragedy occurring in women's lives today as they slowly buckle under the crushing pressure of trying to do it all, have it all, and be all things to all people. The stress of it drives many women to heavy drinking or antidepressants to numb the pain just so they can get through to fight another day.

Simply put, the solution is to acknowledge the deep effect of growing up in a praise and criticism cycle. It's not your fault. It's not your parent's fault. When we share our dreams and ideas with our family and friends, it's natural to want an encouraging and warm reception. We would of course welcome approval and reassurance, but consider this for a moment. Can your friends and family really know if your ideas are feasible? Can your best friend know whether your career transition will work out for you? Can a parent or guardian really know if your plans to explore a business idea will be successful?

What we'd all like to hear is something like, "It's wonderful that you're looking to change your career path. How can you gain insight into the skills and qualities that will make you a successful candidate for your new position?" More likely, you'll hear a straight, "I think that's a good idea," or "I think that's a bad idea," or "I'm not sure about that idea." When people hear your idea, most of them immediately think about why they would or wouldn't do what you're thinking of doing. Others' opinions — the praise or criticism — doesn't tell you about you; it tells you about them.

How about if you looked at it like this? When you want to transition to a new field of interest, or you have an idea for an entrepreneurial endeavor or innovation, employers or leaders in that field are the ones who would have relevant and valuable opinions about what you want to do. These are the people whose opinion might be able to give you the information you need to make your decision.

The most influential person you will ever meet in your life is You

I remember thinking for a very long time that I would be *found*, that someone huge would see something special in me, I'd get a huge deal and everything would be perfect in my life. At the time of writing, I am 48 and Tressarn said something to me about five years ago that changed my life: *"The most influential person you will ever meet in your life is you."* Never were truer words spoken and it's as true for you as it is for me.

After the *be yourself* experience by the elevator in Miami in 2016, I started to be the most influential person in my life. **I stopped feeding the praise and criticism cycle that had me trapped for much of my life, and I started helping other women to do the same.** I continue doing that here, leading by example. I encourage you to show up as your true self, the true self you know you are and who is excited for all the things you want to be. The world then sees you as the woman you are in life — unburdened by self-doubt and free from their long-standing cycle of praise and criticism

We'll talk more on this later, but for now, it's worth taking a moment to ask yourself the hard questions.

Life Purpose Check-in Exercise

Self Assessment

Before we proceed with the rest of the book, let's first check in with where you are in relation to how you feel about the opinion of others.

Below, rate yourself on a scale from 1 — 10 on how accurate the statements are —1 means "not accurate at all," and 10 means "most accurate."

Once you've rated yourself for each statement, total up your scores, then use the Answer Key to determine your next steps.

Channel of Clarity Method

What Others Think Check-in	Self Rating
I make my feelings known.	
I am happy to say what I want.	
I always speak my mind.	
I take the initiative in my life.	
I don't need anyone's approval but my own.	
I never change myself to make another happy.	
I find it easy to say No to people.	
I love taking responsibility for decision making.	
I am ok with people not agreeing with me.	
I am comfortable to share a contrary opinion with my loved ones.	
My Score:	

What Your Score Really Means

Score: 10 — 24
Highly influenced by Others

With a score this low, you likely spend a lot of time trying to keep other people happy. You probably get stuck in your head, trying to work out what you can do or say to avoid criticism. You're likely to experience confusion about what you really think, can flip-flop your opinions with each person you talk to, and have a hard time making decisions.

It doesn't have to be that way, if you want it to change.

To course-correct and find your true purpose in life, free from the opinions of others, you'll find that discovering your unique life purpose strengths will give you the confidence to be yourself — regardless of who is with you.

Score: 25 — 74
Become More Than a Silent Observer

You have your own thoughts and feelings and you are currently avoiding the opinions of others by remaining silent about your deepest wants and needs. This remaining silent, stunts your ability to grow and fully explore your true purpose. Your dreams for yourself and your life are secrets only explored like a fantasy that will never become real. Your sense of wanting more from life makes you feel too vulnerable to share — especially as it is so elusive and difficult to explain to others.

Sadly, such an approach won't sustain you for long. You only get more unhappy and more resentful about denying the dreams you hold inside that you are too afraid to make a reality.

Instead, it's time for you to get crystal clear on your true life purpose and the unique strengths that will get you there, free from the opinion of others. Learning how to find and follow your true purpose path *no matter what* others might say, provides a very different outcome from staying silent your whole life and never living the life you came to live.

Channel of Clarity is the exact system that can help you find your true purpose in life, discover your unique strengths, and receive crystal clear life purpose guidance every step of the way to guarantee you live your true purpose. Your job now is to integrate the dreams you hold inside into your daily life. This book's methods accelerate your results and show you and everyone else that you have what it takes.

Score: 75+
Time For the Life You Deserve

You are already doing what's necessary to overcome your fear of criticism and the opinions of others, but now you need to get specific life purpose guidance in a way that means you can get to live your true purpose in life.

Channel of Clarity is the fastest path to doing exactly that.

Because you've already mastered the art of free thinking and have an independent mind, living the life you deserve will be a breeze. You'll have access to clear life purpose guidance, which means that just by being you, you'll be able to live your true life purpose at an unusually accelerated rate.

Remember, having your own mind is what got you here, it's what will get you there, and it's the only way to live the full life purpose you deserve. Without your independent mind, you'd fall back to square one. Trust me, it's easier for you to live your true purpose than to accept less than you want and deserve.

Life Purpose Block 3 : Prioritising the Needs of Others

I'd like to address a deeply hidden and unspoken block to finding your true purpose in life — learning to ignore your own needs and putting the needs of others first. **Somewhere along the way, women often get swallowed up by believing that it is selfish to take me time.** Many are taught their needs are less important than the needs of others, so they learn to ignore their own needs and put others' needs first.

Countless women are running the entire show, from home life to the workplace, regularly prioritising everyone else's needs. For them, focussing on themselves, giving themselves time to do what they love, seems almost impossible. Numerous women give their energy to other's welfare every waking moment, working hard to feel valued: overhelping; overdoing; giving of themselves and ending the day drained. Is this a first-hand experience for you?

Prioritising your own needs can be truly challenging

When you have been conditioned since childhood to tend to others' needs first, that destructive behaviour gets ingrained in your psyche then is reinforced by societal expectations of women. When you were a little girl, you learned about right and wrong from family members, especially parents. When you did something your parents considered wrong, they expressed disappointment and it usually carried a disciplinary consequence. Disappointing a parent typically triggers feelings of guilt or regret. **Then, wanting to win back their approval, you correct your behaviour and do what they wanted you to do.** All around us we see women prioritising the needs of others, in order to avoid feeling *bad* or *wrong*, in keeping with what they learned in their childhoods.

Breaking the habit of prioritising others

It's possible to become an extremely popular individual by putting the needs of others first. You'll be called kind and supportive and other pleasing names. Being kind does feel good when it is freely offered; however, when you are continuously generous, others can come to expect your kindness. Your name is automatically added to projects without consulting you or colleagues raise their hand on your behalf saying, "She'll do it — she always does." **Feelings of resentment can rise within you when your kindness is expected and your willingness is assumed.** Suddenly, your choice to give is not being respected. Likewise, the habit of being kind can foster the same expectations of ourselves, so we quickly say yes to helping without thinking it through, then resent the time and effort we must expend.

Here's my point: Whether it's work, family, volunteering, or helping friends, it can be incredibly difficult not to put your hand up to offer *more* help.

Why is it so hard to break the cycle of putting everyone else first? One word: **Guilt.** Guilt is an unpleasant feeling that plays on our sense of right and wrong and our sense of responsibility according to the morals of our culture. From birth, we are surrounded by conscious and unconscious ideas of what is expected of us as members of our society. Failing to live up to that ideal — not living up to our responsibilities, doing something wrong, or not doing something perceived as the right thing to do — can leave us feeling guilty, that we are lacking in some way, or that we are failures. Those feelings can be so strong that it is almost impossible for us to say no to whatever is being asked of us. It isn't always easy to understand why we feel guilty and few are taught how to deal with feelings of guilt. **Many women, however, have erroneous guilt. They feel guilty about things for which they are not responsible.**

Clients have told me they feel guilty over actions they see as *bad* or *wrong* that relate directly to prioritising their own needs. Women, especially, find themselves constantly seeking to avoid such feelings of selfishness and the ensuing guilt, so they take steps to correct their *mistakes*, and continue the expected acts of kindness in an effort to reduce those guilty feelings, even though the relief is temporary.

Women are easily guilt-tripped

According to the Oxford English Dictionary, a guilt trip is defined as things that are said to impose feelings of guilt on someone. The main ways to do this are through emotional or psychological pressure. Making choices motivated by avoiding feeling guilty, sets you up to be manipulated easily by others. Subtle comments or body language are often enough to lay a guilt trip that pressures you into doing what others want you to do. Over and over again, your guilty feelings can motivate you to make a situation better, to meet others' expectations, or to give others' needs priority. This cycle of guilt and prioritising leads to chronic guilt, which leads further to deep feelings of inadequacy. Feelings of guilt have led women to live lives with an inability to value or prioritise themselves.

The field of psychology is rife with studies about the causes and effects of guilt and guilt complexes. **Silently suffering from persistently feeling guilty over wrongs you believe you caused or could cause, results in a paralysing fear of doing something wrong.** It is debilitating to believe you are always making mistakes and can't do anything right. Such fears make your world small and your experience of life limited. Once women understand that guilt is a conditioned emotion, one that is learned, they can begin the transformation to a larger life based in freedom, choice, and personal growth.

I'm not trying to make you feel uncomfortable. I want you to be completely free to live your true purpose in life and that the guilt and exhaustion caused by doing everything for everyone else become a distant memory.

Let me ask you a straightforward question. What would happen to you, and ultimately those closest to you, if you became too physically ill to continue to be the one who does everything for everyone else? What if you woke up tomorrow and couldn't type, couldn't speak, or couldn't run around being the one that makes everything work? Scary thought, right?

Prioritising the needs of others is a scary way to live your life. **Your life has immeasurable value and you are here to live a life of joy and purpose.** If you constantly defer your needs in favour of others' to feel valuable, knowing your life purpose path will show you that **this is not *living* your life purpose.** Living a full life is so much more.

A life truly lived is positive and uplifting, something that is very different from just going through the motions from day to day — very different indeed. Let me give you an example of a client's life to show the contrast.

Jen came to me because she had, so to speak, painted herself into a painful corner in her life. Jen is a wife and mother who works hard and long hours in the medical field. Jen describes herself as strong and capable and admits to being always on output. She is a loving wife and mother. She cares deeply about the people in her life and she's a reliable and supportive friend. Jen works hard in her career and gives her best to her work and colleagues every day.

Problems started for Jen when she was in her late 30s. She felt tired all of the time. A few little health issues cropped up, tummy aches and headaches, but she soldiered on as she believed a strong and capable woman would.

Jen's menopause began in her 40s and she felt like her body was rebelling. She put on weight and started to feel what she described as irrational anxiety. Jen found that coping with daily life and her emotions was exhausting. An even bigger issue was that she had built her life based on other people's needs. Jen's struggles with daily life were a symptom of her buckling under the pressure of a lifetime of putting everyone else first.

Jen suffered from chronic guilt. This began when she was a little girl. Born into a family who had great expectations of her and held her to high standards, she had towed the line and followed a path in life that would make her parents happy and proud of her. She grew up feeling guilty about actions they would see as bad or wrong, which meant she prioritised their needs, including their validation of themselves by her acting as they expected her to act. This led to constantly seeking to avoid feelings of guilt and taking steps to correct her mistakes when she strayed from meeting others' needs or expectations. The acts of doing things for others temporarily eased her feelings of guilt. Jen could not imagine how to prioritise her own needs without being considered selfish — a definite wrong according to the moral code she had internalized. This all changed with getting to know her guardian angel.

Jen and I worked closely together with her guardian angel to find and follow her life purpose path. Jen reports that she feels healthier and happier today than she remembers ever feeling. She is happy, too, about fitting into the clothes that have been hiding away in her wardrobe for when she'd be slim again. **Jen's life purpose path has aligned her, her relationships, and her work harmoniously.** She's doing her best work, enjoying her best relationships, and living a life where her needs are met. She is loving life.

Jen worried for many years about what would happen if she could no longer do all that she was doing. Now she knows that, if she were to become physically incapable of doing anything in her life tomorrow, her home would still function perfectly well. Everyone at work would know what to do. None of it would require her to micromanage or deliver instructions from her sick bed!

So, here are a couple of questions:

1. How can she be so sure that's what would happen?

2. How exactly did she get there as a wife, mother, working in a high-pressure setting, with a history of overhelping and a guilt complex?

First off, she focuses on her life purpose path, aligning and harmonising the dynamics of her life, her relationships, and her work. Doing things for everyone else is no longer her priority. She knows what her life purpose path is and following it guides her with a constant peaceful flow, day in and day out.

Jen has chosen this life method:
ACTION: Follow my life purpose path
RESULT: I do what I love to do every day — without guilt

For Jen, the action of following her life purpose path has become completely normal. Having chosen this process once, it now is her life 24/7 and guides her choices from day to day.

Now, that all sounds lovely, but looking at where you are today, you might think such a thing is *impossible* — and, without a process to follow, you'd likely be right. To follow your true life purpose path, you need a method for knowing what that path is and that can guide you each day along the way.

Constantly trying to make everyone else's life work well, besides consuming a lot of your energy, makes it difficult to focus on finding your true purpose in life. Even knowing what you want to do, doing what you love in life is extra challenging if you are constantly distracted by others' needs.

I'd like to leave you with this analogy to illustrate the point I am making about the vital importance of prioritising your own needs. When you board a flight, just before take-off the flight attendant explains all the important information about safety on the flight. They always remind their passengers that, if an emergency situation occurs, you must put your own oxygen mask on first, before attempting to help those around you. Such an action may be counter-intuitive because of our social conditioning to feel selfish if you attend to your own needs before the needs of others. That is far from the truth and the reasoning is sound. By attending to yourself first, you *are* more able to attend to others.

Because you are a woman who can offer much value to the world, people will continue to ask for your help, call you for answers, or ask you for input and support. How can you possibly be all that you want to be for others, if you are not meeting your own needs first? You can only be what you want to be for others by making sure you are whole — physically, mentally, emotionally, and spiritually.

I want you to be free to find and follow your life purpose path so you can live your best life, in all areas. This book shows you how and lets you see how simply it can be done.

Life Purpose Check-in Exercise

Self Assessment

Before we proceed with the rest of the book, let's check in with where you're at right now with prioritising your needs.

Below, rate yourself on a scale from 1 — 10 on how accurate the statements are —1 means "not accurate at all," and 10 means "most accurate."

Once you've rated yourself for each statement, total up your scores, then use the Answer Key to determine your next steps.

Prioritising the Needs of Others Check-in	Self Rating
I reflect on my own needs, desires, and dreams.	
I have a self-care routine.	
I actively look for ways to make time for myself.	
I deserve better than coming second or less, I know I do.	
I take time for myself.	
I value my time.	
I have clear boundaries with others.	
I feel respected by others.	
I am comfortable asking others for help.	
I always take care of myself first and foremost.	
My Score:	

What Your Score Really Means

> **Score: 10 — 28**
> **Your Dreams are a Distant Memory**

Right now, you are putting the needs of others not just before your own needs — but *instead* of your own needs. You are likely unaware of what your own needs are, and your desires and dreams are a distant memory.

You are likely feeling stuck with a millstone around your neck of duties and finding yourself tied to responsibilities in other people's lives. There's no thought for yourself, no feeling of excitement for your future, no peace, and, likely, little-to-no energy left for yourself.

The good news is, it can only get better. And, luckily, the process for getting better is to do less, not more. More is what got you into this situation in the first place. As impossible as it sounds, knowing your life purpose path and having the right guidance to live it, opens up time for you that is invisible to you right now: time for a change, time for you. There is time to live your true purpose in life and experience a way of living that improves the lives of everyone you care about, starting with your own. **Channel of Clarity** is the how.

Score: 29 — 63
It's Time for You

You are teaching people how to treat you by what you are allowing in your relationships. You highly value being loyal, honest and supportive. You care about being the person others can turn to for help when they are having difficulties. You consider yourself to be kind and giving, but you'll be caught in a prioritising-guilt cycle in your life. Your own health, happiness are being neglected in favour of the needs of others. You are so busy prioritising the needs of others that your own dreams and desires are very much on the back burner.

Right now, your main focus should be actively making time for yourself and your own life. Focus on pouring your energy into finding and following your true purpose in life and put your own dreams and desires front and centre.

The only way you'll live the life you came for — your true life purpose — is with a method that allows you to receive all the life purpose guidance and help you'll ever need to get you there.

I can promise that your life will never be the same once you've experienced what it's like to receive crystal clear life purpose guidance from your guardian angel, and the to realise that you can create life together with your guardian angel.

Score: 64+
Your True Purpose Awaits

It's time, now, for you to make your way to your true purpose in life. **Channel of Clarity** is a method of finding and following your life purpose path with all the help from your guardian angel that you'll ever need.

Many of our clients have found that focusing on their true purpose in life with their guardian angel has given them immediate peace and a depth of fulfillment that they have been longing for, for their entire lives.

You have good boundaries, you know the value of developing yourself and constantly becoming the best version of yourself — for you and for those you care about.

Channel of Clarity is simply the way to know your purpose and have your guardian angel give you all the support you need to live your true purpose in life. As soon as you get it implemented, you can enjoy the experience of life with a source of crystal clear guidance along the way to living the life you came to live.

Key Chapter Takeaways

- **Life Purpose Block #1. Fear and Self Doubt**

    Self doubt is the primary Life Purpose Block because the more you doubt yourself, the more fearful and self-critical you become, and the less progress you make in life. The cost of women's self-doubt is beyond measure. Think of all the ideas unshared, businesses not started, and talents unused. Many women find self-doubt surfaces most intensely around their deepest felt hopes and dreams. **Self-doubt not only distracts you from making progress, it also eats your dreams**.

- **Life Purpose Block #2. What Others Think**

    It is understandable to want to know we are appreciated and valued. However, that is not what should be running your life. **So many women never talk about their accomplishments and prevent their own success in order to avoid being the target of praise**. For your health and well-being, detach from both the dependency on others' praise and the fear of their disapproval.

- **Life Purpose Block #3. Prioritising the Needs of Others**

    Countless women are running the entire show, from home life to the workplace, regularly prioritising everyone else's needs. Whether it's work, family, volunteering, or helping friends, it can be incredibly difficult not to put your hand up to offer *more* help. **Many women, however, have erroneous guilt. They feel guilty about things for which they are not responsible.** If you constantly defer your needs in favour of others' to feel valuable, knowing your life purpose path shows you that this is not *living* your life purpose.

Ros Place

Chapter 4

Your Guardian Angel is the Key

"Trusting our intuition often saves us from disaster."
-Anne Wilson Schaef

I have worked with women for more than 18 years, solving the puzzle of what leads a woman, at any stage of her life, to live her true life purpose, especially at the highest and most fulfilling level. How can I take a woman from, *"I don't know what my purpose is or even where to start,"* all the way to, *"Wow, if I'd known it was this good, I'd have done it years ago"*?

Working with hundreds of women and their guardian angels has taught me this, so far. Every woman needs to answer three life purpose questions clearly and accurately before she can find and follow her life purpose path. In later chapters, we'll explore your connection with your guardian angel and I'll show you how to have a relationship with them that answers these questions in profound ways. For now, let's explore the three life purpose questions.

Three Life Purpose Questions

Question #1. What if I'm the *only* woman without a life purpose?

As a woman looking for more happiness in life, it's natural to have a certain amount of hesitancy about truly exploring your life purpose. It might surface within you as a feeling of doubt, trepidation, second-guessing, or a lack of self-confidence. You might find yourself dragging your feet and worrying about what you might discover about yourself.

I've known clients to say, jokingly, "What if I'm the *only* one in the world who doesn't have a life purpose?!" Women often feel this uncertainty, because of deep-seated feelings of inadequacy, often feeling as if you are not enough. They've felt humiliated or rejected in the past and want to prepare themselves for what they consider to be the inevitable fail. Women are more prone to feeling doubt about having a life purpose because of unconscious ideologies of women's lower value in society, something that is affirmed through gender inequity in pay, opportunities, cultural norms, and value derived from prioritising others instead of themselves. With such ingrained feelings, it's hard for them to believe they are alive to contribute to the world in a meaningful way — purely by being their unique self. Doubt is a natural experience when you find yourself at the edge of the unknown.

I promise you, you have a life purpose. And you have a guardian angel that exists purely to support and guide you along its path. Your guardian angel is the most empowering, positive, and natural guide to learning how to believe in yourself, your purpose, and the life you have come here to live.

Your guardian angel's sole purpose is to love, empower, and be with you in this lifetime, to remind you of who you came to be, and to support and guide you to find and follow your life purpose. They exist exclusively for you as your life purpose guide.

Your guardian angel is a powerful catalyst for belief change. When your beliefs change, they carry a tremendous amount of momentum towards action. It manifests itself as excitement, commitment, and eagerness — suddenly your path becomes clear. Connecting with your guardian angel, makes you able to tap into your true purpose and start to live the life of your dreams.

Guardian angel connections are transformative within **Channel of Clarity**, partly because they validate what you have always hoped was true about yourself. That validation opens you up to your truth and activates your hidden potential. I want you to see the power of what your guardian angel can do in every area of your life: the epiphanies it can spark; the radical way it can transform your entire life.

My goal is to welcome you as a client because I would love to help you personally. However, I know the first thing I must do is help you determine whether the **Channel of Clarity** approach is right for you. Will it give you all you need to find and focus on your true life purpose? Will it suit your personality, your life, your goals, your current state of being?

The book you are reading was written holding nothing back, explaining what I know, sharing my passion, and, I hope, inspiring you to make my method part of your life too. Many readers go on to connect with their guardian angel, find their purpose in life, find more peace and happiness, and follow their life purpose path to continue to improve every part of their life. This isn't an accident. I want that for you.

I can't stress enough, your guardian angel is like an ever-present, ever-loving guide whose favourite thing to do is to help you. Your guardian angel never takes vacations. He or she never complains. Your guardian angel guides you towards your life purpose path day in and day out, and loves doing so.

Question #2. Who can I trust to guide me?

Women need to know they can trust both the source and the accuracy of the information they are receiving. Trust is an essential quality that is often hard to find and easy to lose. Many of my clients needed to establish or reestablish a sense of trust in their lives. Lots of women have been wounded by abuse, betrayal, or loss in their lives. Even those who have been spared such trauma find themselves growing into womanhood with confusion caused by mixed messages from others. Lies and disappointments can damage our trust in others and in ourselves.

Without trust, life is scary. A looming sense or fear of crisis complicates and confuses our decision making. Choosing to learn to trust sees you consciously moving away from fear and back into your heart where trust and truth reside. This creates the safe, secure, and confident *knowing* that guides you honestly.

For many women, the greatest damage to trust has come at times when they were most vulnerable. **Fear of being judged negatively makes many women resist asking for help and be reluctant to open up to others at the best of times, and when they have, the reactions**

they encounter often leave them feeling betrayed and empty. It is a particularly bitter pill to take when the trust they place in a professional is not honoured. For example, unfortunately, mentoring and coaching situations have resulted in considerable pain for many women when mentors they placed their trust in did not provide support or, even worse, exploited their vulnerability, betrayed, or undermined them. Hierarchical mentor—mentee relationships can be particularly tricky.

Fears and emotional wounds from the past can lead women to trust others unwisely, rashly, or without thorough consideration. On the other hand, conscious or unconscious fears can create a defence mechanism around the heart that leads some women to refuse to trust anyone, no matter how trustworthy they may be. Neither pattern leads women to find more peace or develop more trust.

Contrary to what you might think, first and foremost it is essential to learn to trust yourself. Your guardian angel helps you trust in yourself and that gives you the courage and capability to create meaningful and lasting changes in your life.

For women I work with, their relationships with their guardian angels have been the piece of validation that allows them to trust in themselves and that empowers them to make choices that are right for them. They cherish their relationship with their guardian angel, because it allows them to experience a sacred partnership, unlike any other in their lives. They see that their relationship with their guardian angel has made them a better friend, lover, parent or acquaintance.

What your guardian angel does better than mentoring, coaching, or therapy routes is they deliver information to you — in a way that you can instantly validate. Validating your thoughts, feelings and choices for yourself, helps you know that you can be trusted.

Many exercises in this book are designed to help you uncover and heal trust in yourself. For example, later in this book we will be doing some validation of the **Channel of Clarity** itself through exercises, client case studies, and other information. These exercises and information help you consider the information that I've laid out.

Think back to the early part of this book where I asked you to take the Life Purpose Check-ins. Did any light bulbs go off? Were you able to see yourself in the answers? As a result, do you have a clearer awareness of yourself?

This book has been written with the kind blessing of many of my clients and their guardian angels. My guardian angel, Tressarn, is writing with me. We want to give you what you need to validate the information I am providing. I know how important it is to feel trust, so I have created repeated opportunities for you to build trust in yourself and in this proposed method of finding your life purpose path.

The true joy of my work is seeing you find trust in yourself and in offering ways for you to find proof that confirms what you are coming to know about yourself and your abilities. Developing that trust, gives you a strong foundation from which to build your relationship with your guardian angel. Communicating with your guardian angel is a way to continue to validate your truth as you learn, grow, and live with their unconditional love and support.

In later chapters, I'm going to teach you how to connect with your guardian angel, discover and validate your unique life purpose strengths and communicate with your guardian angel in ways that continue to validate your truth.

Your connection with your guardian angel is a sacred partnership that guides you towards your true purpose in life and supports you every step of the way.

Question #3. Is this right for me?

One of the by-products of a relationship with your guardian angel is knowing the truth.

As I have said, my guardian angel, Tressarn, is helping me share information with you about the **Channel of Clarity**, and we are not holding back on anything. For example, in the next chapter you'll read about the reasons you might not want to connect with your guardian angel. I'm here to show you the pros and cons. I can do this because, again, I have no secret agenda for what happens as a result of you reading this book. My number one goal is to create a book of value, so I can help many more women find their true purpose. If you like this book enough to share it with a few friends, and those friends share it, and they share it, etc., then anything less than the truth would be unconscionable because it would mislead many people, betray your trust, and, essentially, be contrary to my purpose — so, I hold nothing back.

Channel of Clarity takes care of moving you from connection with your guardian angel to finding and following your true life purpose path. Because of all the ways your guardian angel guides you to your purpose in life, I want to be upfront and realistic about the other options you have. Besides valuing honesty and integrity, there are several reasons why I am choosing to present this information to you in this way:

1. I connect hundreds of women with their guardian angels every year, so there are limits to my time. I take on four private clients a month and one or two group coaching clients per day.

2. My work with guardian angels is unique and impossible to find anywhere else. Holding back on sharing information with you devalues what I've struggled to develop over long hours, months, and even longer years.

3. I want to tell you what your options are, because I want to be your first choice. I want to work with women who are 100% committed to finding and following their life purpose path. The care and dedication I give to the women I work with is too valuable to waste. I want to work with women who want to work with me. Giving you options lets you make an informed choice about working with me.

For me, being open and honest in this book, showing you how I can help you communicate with your guardian angel to find your life purpose, is the best way for me to connect with the right women.

Think of it this way:

I want to help as many women as possible to connect with their guardian angel and find and follow their life purpose path. My guardian angel, Tressarn, is helping me to do so, helping me to communicate with the women who are ready for my help.

If a woman comes to me asking about helping them to find and follow their life purpose path and then says, *"I need to do a bit more research,"* comes to me for a second time and says, *"I'm still looking at options,"* comes to me a third time and says, "*I just need to talk to one more person before I make a move forward,*" comes to me for a fourth time etc., etc... **How productive is that process when they could have learned all of their options, given in full and honest transparency, inside this book?**

I am passionate about efficiency. The past 48 years seem to have flashed before my very eyes and I want to help as many women as possible to find and follow their life purpose path. Wasting time in communication with people who *"still need to do research"* is not a good use of anyone's time.

I can tell you that, ever since I shared **Channel of Clarity** with women, I have very little communication where women ask for multiple delays to do more research. I believe that I have a moral and ethical duty to provide you with all you need here, so you *know* if this is a good fit and can make a choice that is right for you.

If this past few years has taught us anything, **you never know what tomorrow will bring, so make positive changes today.**

As you begin to consider finding your true purpose in life, it's natural to ask yourself more questions to find out if this is right for you. Let's look at some examples of questions I am commonly asked, so you can test for yourself to see the power of your guardian angel and the kinds of miracles they can work.

Questions I am Commonly Asked

#1. Will I find out good things about myself?

Many women seem much more aware of their shortcomings than their strengths. As a woman, I believe there is a certain humility that comes with knowing my weaknesses and accepting that I am very far from being perfect. It is also my own experience that such analysing can soon get out of hand. I see many women respond with self-deprecating comments when faced with a compliment. I see many women unable to say 'thank you' when sincere appreciation is communicated to them. It's a struggle for many women to believe that they bring value to the lives of others. **It's hard for many women to see the good things about themselves, so they spend a lifetime oblivious to their strengths.**

It's not enough to tell a woman what her strengths are. She must see them for herself, and recognize them as her truth, the essence of who she is. You may have experienced this for yourself when trying to help a friend going through a crisis of faith in herself. You see how incredible a person she is, yet the more you tell her what you appreciate and admire about her, the more she digs into the limiting way she sees herself.

Connecting with your guardian angel reveals the good things about you, the things you have been gifted with, and shows you your valuable strengths in a way that you can see for yourself. Likewise, your relationship with your guardian angel is a strength-based approach to finding your life purpose, which occurs by revealing the assets you naturally possess. Once your guardian angel lays out your strengths in front of you, you can see yourself as they see you. You, finally, will discover the truth of all of the good things about you and the revelation will change your approach to life, entirely.

Whatever you are looking to achieve in your life, you were born with strengths that will support you in doing so. Imagine living your life based on the confidence that you have what you need to accomplish any goal you choose.

#2. What can I expect from my life purpose path?

In one word — pleasure.

Often, I work with women who expect the exact opposite — pain. Many women I work with have developed a tendency towards martyrdom and constantly doing for others. What you can expect from this approach is letting the process of finding and following your life purpose be *easy*.

For many women, myself included, it's a real ask to consider that meaningful improvements or significant accomplishments in life can happen because you are doing things you love, instead of driving yourself into the ground, struggling, and pushing yourself hard as we have been taught is necessary for success. When you are doing things you love, change happens easily. Like many women, I'd come to believe that anything worthwhile could only be achieved through constant drive, willpower, and hard, hard work. **Surprisingly, when I chose to follow my life purpose path it brought more ease and more pleasure into my life.**

Your life purpose is as joyful to pursue as to achieve. It reflects the things you love to do as opposed to what you feel you should do.

Your life purpose path resonates with who you are at your essence and manifests in the spirit of pleasure and enjoyment.

#3. Do I have the time for this?

Here is a last point on why communicating with your guardian angel is the best way to find and follow your life purpose path.

During my 18 years of working with women, the best clients have been leaders. They may not manage a team, but they are leaders nonetheless, whether it be in their own lives, in their families, or in their community. I have also noticed, like many before me, that leaders understand that their success lies in being the best they can be in their lives. I've yet to find a successful woman who doesn't want to become a better person. That means successful women like to spend time in personal development and discovery. Connection with their guardian angel is a great way to reach their highest potential and live the best version of life possible.

Good leaders also acknowledge that they do not accomplish their goals by themselves. A team can be two or more, but it is never just one and every member contributes. Working with your guardian angel taps into the part of good leadership that is being open to working with others. Perhaps this is why many leaders readily connect with their guardian angels and work together to accomplish their goals.

There's just one problem. Women who are leaders are also busy. Really, really busy. They're busy with work, family, and in their community. That is why connection with their guardian angel needs to fit seamlessly into their lives.

Your relationship with your guardian angel fits within the schedule of the most successful and busy women. This makes a connection with your guardian angel convenient and convenient access to the empowerment and bliss of your guardian angel is key to finding and following your life purpose path.

So, if your goal with **Channel of Clarity** is to find your true life purpose it will happen in ways that are time efficient and fit into your daily life like a perfectly fitting glove.

Key Chapter Takeaways

- There are three major questions that all women must have answered before they can find and follow her life purpose path.

- **Question #1. What if I'm the *only* woman without a life purpose?**
  Women are prone to feeling doubt about having a life purpose because of unconscious ideologies of women's lower value in society. I can promise you that you have a life purpose and you have a guardian angel that exists purely to support and guide you along its path.

- **Question #2. Who can I trust to guide me?**
  Women need to know they can trust both the source and the accuracy of the information they are receiving. Many of my clients needed to establish or reestablish a sense of trust in their lives. For the women I work with, their relationships with their guardian angels have been the piece of validation that allows them to trust in themselves and that empowers them to make choices that are right for them.

- **Question #3. Is this right for me?**
  As you begin to consider finding your true purpose in life, it's natural to ask yourself more questions to find out if this is right for you:

  Point #1. Only Good Things: Connecting with your guardian angel reveals the good things about you, the things you have been gifted with, and shows you your valuable strengths in a way that you can see for yourself

  Point #2. Pleasure & Enjoyment: Your life purpose is as joyful to pursue as to achieve. It reflects the things you love to do as opposed to what you feel you should do. Your life purpose path resonates with who you are at your essence and manifests in the spirit of pleasure and enjoyment.

  Point #3. Seamless Fit: Your relationship with your guardian angel fits within the schedule of the most successful and busy women. This makes connection with your guardian angel convenient and convenient access to the empowerment and bliss of your guardian angel is key to finding and following your life purpose path.

Ros Place

Chapter 5

The #1 Problem with Guardian Angel Connection

> *"For me the greatest beauty always lies in the greatest clarity."*
> – *Gotthold Ephraim Lessing*

I love connecting with guardian angels so women can find and follow their life purpose path. Some, however, have tried connecting with their guardian angel and been wildly disappointed in their results. The specific reason for their disappointment is the topic of this chapter.

There is a fundamental problem with some people's expectations of a guardian angel's role in life purpose discovery, which we'll explore here. **Put simply, connecting with your guardian angel alone doesn't lead you to live your life purpose.**

Connecting with your guardian angel is the first step to knowing your life purpose, but you need a way to navigate to successfully follow your life purpose path. Developing your connection with your guardian angel to receive continued guidance and direction is essential for you to live your true life purpose.

It takes time and energy to receive guidance and direction from your guardian angel and it begins with something as simple, and yet vital, as their name. **Your guardian angel's name has a very important life purpose message for you.** You need to know what they look like — you'll discover the importance of your guardian angel's appearance in the coming chapters. You can learn what your unique strengths are and exactly how to use them in your life. You can establish a personal way of asking important questions and be provided with accurate answers.

Many clients have tried other methods to connect with their guardian angels. There are lots of people on the Internet offering to tell you who your guardian angel is. Many women write to tell me that they are confused to have been told by an angel reader that their guardian angel is their grandad in heaven. This is not possible as your guardian angel has never lived a human life.

I am frequently asked to confirm whether, in fact, someone's guardian angel's name really is Michael. Also, people often contact me to check what they have been told by others. A regular event is to be contacted by a dismayed woman who has been given information about her purpose in life that makes no sense and doesn't give her any clarity. There is no inner validation, no resonance of truth. When this happens, I answer by asking some basic questions:

- Were you told your guardian angel's name and why they have this name?

- Do you know what your guardian angel looks like — and what their appearance means?

- Were you told of your unique strengths in life in a way that resonated deeply with your inner truth?

- Were you given messages from your guardian angel that touched your core and validated what you have always known deep inside?

If the answer is no to any of these, you have not connected with your guardian angel.

Imagine the time that these women are wasting, to say nothing of the emotional roller coaster of hope and disappointment they are experiencing. It takes a lot of energy to keep restoring your faith in yourself and others. Think of the soul searching it takes, the hours of introspection, the endless life lessons you feel you need to be learning.

So, if such wasted time and efforts are your reality, and they can be, why am I such a proponent of connecting with your guardian angel?

Well, it's quite simple, actually. **I know how to make a true connection with your guardian angel.**

I know what it looks like, what it feels like, and how it resonates with your inner truth. I know from my own experience and from what I have seen with my clients.

Still, it's just the first step. You have yet to receive the personal guidance and step by step direction you required to follow your life purpose path. The first step is great if you're just curious to know a bit more about yourself but you will need more than a guardian angel reading to satisfy your yearning to live your true life purpose, to open wide the floodgates of life purpose mastery — even if that reading is with me.

Connecting with your guardian angel as part of a personal step-by-step guidance system is the most effective way to live your true life purpose fully, every day.

So, how can your guardian angel provide you with all the personal guidance and step-by-step direction you need?

Unfortunately, it's not as simple as asking your guardian angel to help you every day. Again, the number one problem with connecting with your guardian angel is that you still need a system for leveraging its benefits. For us, that system is the **Channel of Clarity**. This book is all about this system. Your guardian angel can be limited in how they can help you, but this system helps you open up ways they can reach you with their guidance and provide what you want more accurately. Everything in your life can be radically transformed when you communicate with your guardian angel.

In the next chapter, we'll explore the **Channel of Clarity** system to show you how your guardian angel can guide you to your true purpose in life. Please remember that connecting with your guardian angel is only the first step to finding and following your life purpose path. You also need a channel through which your guardian angel can guide you along that path.

Key Chapter Takeaways

- Connecting with your guardian angel alone doesn't lead you to live your life purpose.

- Connecting with your guardian angel is the first step to knowing your life purpose, but you need a way to navigate to successfully follow your life purpose path.

- Connecting with your guardian angel as part of a personal step-by-step guidance system is the most effective way to live your true life purpose fully, every day.

- **Channel of Clarity** is the system that opens up communication so your guardian angel's guidance can reach you. Everything in your life can be radically transformed when you communicate with your guardian angel.

Part 2

The Channel of Clarity Method

Chapter 6

The Celestial Formula

"Clarity precedes success."
– Robin Sharma

Before we dive into the specifics of how to get the life purpose guidance and direction you need from your guardian angel, I want to teach you about a basic concept necessary for guardian angel communication. It is called **The Celestial Formula**.

If your goal is to live your true life purpose, the path to that life is an issue of clear communication, not guesswork. It's a simple step-by-step process that, once you learn it and apply it to all your communications with your guardian angel, will empower you to live your life purpose in a positive and enriching way — every day.

Specifically, The Celestial Formula looks like this:

When you Connect, Communicate, and Cocreate with your guardian angel, living your true life purpose is imminent and guaranteed.

Let's break this down into individual parts of your relationship with your guardian angel.

Connect

To connect with your guardian angel means to know, see, and hear them in a way that makes you feel your togetherness.

No matter how you plan to receive guidance from your guardian angel, whether it is hearing their words or feeling their presence, first you must establish a connection that opens the communication channel. Once the connection is made and the channel is open, guidance can flow naturally between you and your guardian angel.

Your connection with your guardian angel is a special togetherness that allows a natural understanding and closeness. It creates a bond between you that makes your life purpose guidance certain and easy to validate. Through your connection and the closeness of your relationship, your trust can grow and your guardian angel can deliver life purpose guidance to you in ways that you understand most easily. **Every word and each piece of life purpose guidance your guardian angel gives you, can be delivered only if you are connected.** With your connection you develop a knowingness, a familiarity, and a way of being that feels natural and opens you to receiving what your guardian angel is waiting to convey in a variety of ways. Sometimes your guardian angel will want to *show* you something important. Sometimes they will want to *tell* you what your next step is. Your connection with your guardian angel and the trust and togetherness you create, directly affects your ability to find and follow your true purpose in life.

Creating a personal connection with your guardian angel, therefore, is critical, because it is the only way you can receive their personal and detailed life purpose guidance. There are no exceptions.

Communicate

Communication is a straightforward concept. It is the way we express, share, exchange, or impart information and ideas. Communication with your guardian angel is a two-way exchange through which life purpose guidance can be asked for and received. Knowing how to communicate with your guardian angel involves learning how to ask questions clearly, so you get the answers you seek. Unclear communication can leave you waiting and wondering if your request was heard.

Clear communication with your guardian angel is like having a direct line to important messages and guidance. The messages can go beyond your questions to matters you would never have thought to ask about, but developing your ability to communicate with your guardian angel is the only way to receive the clear messages and life purpose guidance you need to live your true purpose.

Cocreate

To cocreate means to engage in an intentional and supportive relationship with your guardian angel — *doing* life together. It is forming a relationship through which you are always unconditionally supported to accomplish your true purpose. Cocreating with your guardian angel means that you are never alone in your endeavours and you have help to do all the things you would like to do so you can follow your life purpose path peacefully and smoothly. Your guardian angel is right by your side every step of the way.

When you cocreate with your guardian angel, the energy of your entire life purpose flows through you and all that you do. You make your life *together*. Your guardian angel's entire reason for being is to help you. When you cocreate, you find contentment and ease of accomplishing the things your heart desires. And, you allow your guardian angel to guide *and* support you in the highest possible way.

Cocreation happens when you have a connection and a way of communicating with your guardian angel to receive life purpose guidance. Cocreation with your guardian angel is the only way for your true life purpose to become your living reality.

For the **Celestial Formula** approach (when you **connect**, **communicate** and **cocreate** with your guardian angel, living your true life purpose is imminent and guaranteed), all you need is to figure out how to connect with your guardian angel, ask them life purpose questions, and live your life purpose together. However, there is a crucial element to that approach, which is why most humans never find their true purpose in life.

To find your true life purpose path, the communication between you must be clear, so you can ask your guardian angel questions *and* receive their answers. The ability to ask the right questions must be learned. A key factor of the **Channel of Clarity** strategy is how to ask the right life purpose questions and how to receive clear answers. In other words, you and your guardian angel cocreate your life purpose by means of a consistent and clear channel of communication.

Let me give you an example. Let's assume that every time you ask a question about your true purpose in life, you get a clear answer that you can apply to your life and see results in real time.

How does that affect your ability to live your true purpose in life?

It's quite simple. For every clear life purpose question you ask your guardian angel, their clear answer accurately guides you, so you increase your ability to follow your life purpose path. You can ask as many questions as you want and get the answers and guidance you need in return.

Why would you want to keep asking your guardian angel questions?

The possibility of asking your guardian angel any number of questions, gives you the opportunity to choose to explore your purpose in one area of your life at a time.

Having such access to an unlimited bounty of life purpose guidance means you can receive personal direction constantly and clearly about every aspect of your entire life. And, the more you ask questions and receive answers, the stronger your connection with your guardian angel becomes. It's a life purpose win-win: the more you ask, the more that is revealed, and the better life gets.

The quality of the questions you ask your guardian angel makes a big difference in the clarity of the answers you receive. You might ask your guardian angel lots of questions in a day, but are they the best questions to get you the guidance you seek? To ask the best questions, you must be clear about what you want to know. Focused questions allow your guardian angel to give the best answers. To reach your goal of finding and following your life purpose path with your guardian angel, *connect, communicate* (ask the best questions you can, and as many of them as possible), and together you will *cocreate* your life.

By using the simple **Celestial Formula** as outlined above, you can successfully live every aspect of your life purpose. It works 100 percent of the time. It allows you to ask the best life purpose questions and receive answers in a way you can understand and apply to your life for real time results. You can see how a clear two-way channel of communication between you and your guardian angel is essential for such an exchange.

Many women miss out in realising their life purpose by not creating a clear channel of communication with their guardian angel and so limit the amount and accuracy of the life purpose guidance they can receive.

Remember:

When you Connect, Communicate and Cocreate with your guardian angel, living your true life purpose is imminent and guaranteed.

The power of the **Channel of Clarity** is that it *optimises* the process of connecting and communicating with your guardian angel. The added beauty of having such clear *conversations* is that you don't have to wait and wonder if your question has been received or if you'll get an answer.

Many spiritual approaches to receiving guidance suggest you send your request out into the Universe and the answer or solution will manifest when the necessary components in the Universe align. It could be months from the time you ask your important question before you get even a hint of an answer. With the **Channel of Clarity**, you get a clear answer within moments of asking your question. This allows a continuous flow of life purpose guidance from your guardian angel. Ultimately, the immediacy and clarity of your answers and guidance l mean you can start living your life purpose without delay.

As an active part of the **Channel of Clarity**, **The Celestial Formula** is limitless in its effect. The guidance you receive often exceeds what you think of to ask. For example, sometimes when I work with a client or communicate with my own guardian angel, I receive pure guidance that does not come from having asked a question. After answering many questions, your guardian angel is clearer about the essence of what you want to know so, without you having to ask, they can offer guidance about matters indirectly related to your life purpose and which move you forward on your life purpose path. Your guardian angel is not limited only to answering your questions and knows when you are ready to receive such guidance..

When you apply **The Celestial Formula**, your meaningful conversations with your guardian angel lead to revelations and epiphanies that would otherwise be hidden forever. Taking that one step further, the revelations or epiphanies can lead you to a whole series of related questions you'd like to ask — and now you can. The two-way clear communication channel facilitates meaningful conversations that abound in their benefits: you receive real time guidance, answers to every question, and important messages about your life purpose. Such ongoing meaningful conversations are what lead you to live your true life purpose in the most direct way. That is why **The Celestial Formula** is an integral part of the **Channel of Clarity.**

Remember, when you connect, communicate, and cocreate with your guardian angel, living your true life purpose is imminent and guaranteed. Let's recap how it works:

- Connect — know, see, hear, feel togetherness with your guardian angel;
- Communicate — share and exchange life purpose information through a two-way channel with your guardian angel; and

Channel of Clarity Method

- Cocreate — engage in an intentional and supportive relationship with your guardian angel to find, follow, and live your true life purpose.

I cannot overstate the importance of this channel because it makes the communication so clear. The primary goal of the **Channel of Clarity** is to facilitate all communication between you and your guardian angel, regardless of the depth of guidance you want to receive. And, it does so without any frustrating communication lag as used to happen with overseas calls. You talk there's a long silence, you talk again and as you're talking the voice of the person on the other end arrives and you find yourselves talking over each other and not understanding one another. Such communication becomes confusing and muddled because of the time delay between asking a question and getting the answer. Life could easily have moved and your question may not be as relevant as when you asked, if you had to wait days — or longer — to receive your guidance.

The Channel of Clarity method is so effective in today's busy world because of its lack of delays and frustration. You can ask questions easily. You can get answers easily, and together with your guardian angel you receive all the support and guidance you need to live your life purpose, easily.

Now that you understand the basic process that drives this unique method to finding and following your life purpose path and, with your guardian angel, living the life you came to live, let's look at what the **Channel of Clarity** looks like, specifically. In the following pages, I walk you through the exact process and strategies to follow to live your life purpose successfully. At first glance, the moving pieces might seem intimidating, especially if you are new to the concept of guardian angel communication; however, don't let initial impressions keep you from the long-term benefits that this method can provide.

Additionally, you wouldn't be here if you didn't know there was more to life than what you are currently living. Embrace that now, and realise that to achieve something new, something different has to take place.

I am excited to share with you in the next chapter, the step-by-step process that creates a clear channel of communication between you and your guardian angel.

> ## Key Chapter Takeaways
>
> - **The Celestial Formula**: When you Connect, Communicate and Cocreate with your guardian angel, living your life purpose is imminent and guaranteed.
>
> - When you apply **The Celestial Formula**, your meaningful conversations with your guardian angel lead to revelations and epiphanies that would otherwise be hidden forever.

Chapter 7

Creating Your Channel of Clarity Step by Step

"Little by little, one walks far."
– Peruvian Proverb

Channel of Clarity is so named because I want to attract women serious about channeling their guardian angel and receiving clear life purpose guidance. There is an increasing interest in channeling and I want people to know that this is something you can learn to do. I want you to ask, *"Why not me?"* I also want to be upfront and transparent that this method requires communicating with your guardian angel. I'm attracting women who are willing to put in the work it takes to develop clear communication for life purpose guidance. The name matters, and all these factors were taken into consideration. Don't rush trying to connect with your guardian angel. Get help if you need it.

In this book I am sharing with you how I help my clients. I'm sharing what I care deeply about, and what Tressarn and I are committed to teaching. <u>**It is as simple as that.**</u> Throughout the next few chapters,

I want to give you some tools that you can use to start connecting today with your guardian angel.

A fun thing about **Channel of Clarity** is that once you start, the path leads straight to connecting with your guardian angel and discovering your true purpose in life. Often, as soon as I help my clients make the connection with their guardian angel, they immediately see their true purpose. I see my clients' eyes light up as they see purpose throughout all of their life.

As they follow their life purpose path, my clients find all areas of their life improve. Their relationship with their guardian angel makes them a better friend, lover, parent, acquaintance, employee, employer, entrepreneur, or creator.

This section explains each step required to create your Channel of Clarity and facilitate all communication between you and your guardian angel. Before exploring the function and purpose of each step towards creating your direct line of communication, let's take a bird's-eye view of the steps along the way.

This simple four-step process allows us to create the **Channel of Clarity.** If the concepts in this process seem unfamiliar to you, don't worry. The concepts and steps will soon become clear to you.

Let's focus on the function of each of the steps, discover the reasoning behind their order, and their purpose.

Once you have followed the process and established a Channel of Clarity, you can ask yourself these key questions to assess the effectiveness of your Channel of Clarity:

- Do you have a clear connection with your guardian angel?

- Are you communicating effectively with your guardian angel?
- Are you doing life together with your guardian angel?

If you can answer in the affirmative, you have a successful Channel of Clarity between you and your guardian angel.

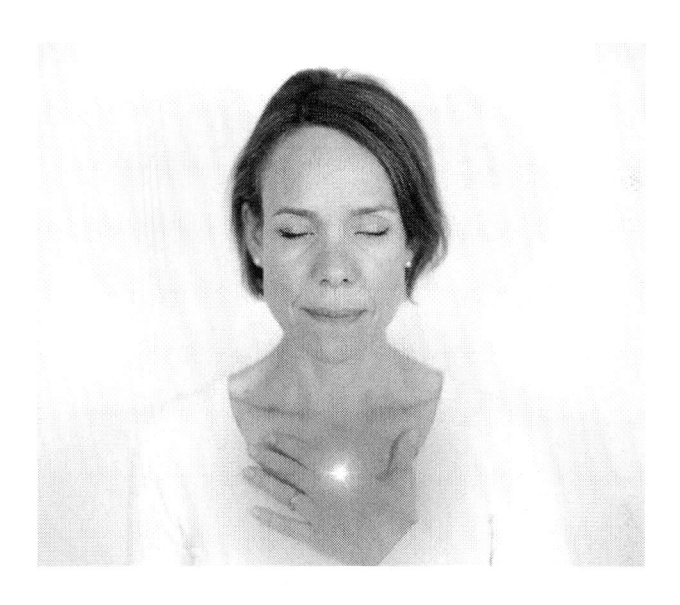

Step #1. Heart Centre State

Place your hand on your upper chest with your thumb just below your collarbone. Beneath your palm is your heart centre. Your heart centre is the centre of truth and love within you. We have all been wounded in the past and have experienced pain in our lives. Many of my clients have experienced trauma and pain that has closed their hearts. Some hold the belief that closing their heart protects them from experiencing further pain in their lives. The reality is that it prevents us from knowing the love that will guide, keep you safe, and even heal the pain. Too many hearts are closed and asleep.

When Tressarn and I began our journey to show women how to find and follow their true purpose, he was very clear that we would begin by awakening the heart centre, and, that it would be effective through its gentleness.

Think of your own experience of waking from sleep. Most people appreciate a gentle awakening and greeting by life. I, myself, find that I awake much happier and more alert when I wake up naturally without the jolt of an alarm. This natural awakening is similar to the experience of awakening your heart centre. Tressarn calls this the heart centre state. When our hearts open because they feel safe and ready, and can do so in their own way, without any pressure or rush, they open naturally and the awakening is of your choosing. Your heart opens to the love it has chosen to receive. You experience love on your terms and in the precise way you wish to receive it. Imagine a beautiful flower opening to warm sunlight, one petal at a time. There is no forcing a flower to bloom, no telling it to bloom in a certain way, no pushing it to bloom without sunlight, no rushing it to be ready before it is ready.

The heart centre state is the first step to creating your Channel of Clarity and living your true life purpose. As your heart centre is naturally awakened you feel yourself effortlessly lifted into a fully functioning state of pure contentment and love. With each revisiting of the heart centre state with your guardian angel, your connection with your guardian angel becomes more familiar, more natural, stronger and more developed.

This first step to creating your Channel of Clarity is simply opening your heart. It is fundamental and creates a connection with your guardian angel that is natural and familiar. You'll also notice that this particular step starts from the centre of love and truth within you — your heart centre. The journey to find and follow your life purpose path must start with love. As I mentioned earlier in this book, your life purpose path begins when you do what you love to do. However, you do not need to be *doing* or even *know* what it is that you love to do before you start to awaken your heart centre. Often, the clients who have completely lost touch with or forgotten the things they love to do have the fastest benefits from experiencing the love of the heart centre state.

Regardless of how awake your heart currently is, your heart centre state is the first and most important step in the process of creating your Channel of Clarity. The more you connect with your guardian angel when in your heart centre state, the more you will know, feel, see, and hear them. Your heart centre state is the one place where you can create the connection with your guardian angel and make the **Celestial Formula** work for you. In turn, you can engage more in the intentional relationship required to live your true purpose in life.

Hidden Treasures

After mentoring my clients to enter their heart centre state, I received reports from them about huge improvements in their lives, even at this first stage of creating their channel with their guardian angel. As the heart centre awakens, love for themselves grows, too. They reported feeling instantly calmer and more peaceful. Another common side effect of the heart centre state they described as a feeling of wanting to smile and of seeing their entire life in clearer ways. Clients report instant improvements in their relationships and that they experience a feeling of ease in daily life as they create their connection with their guardian angel.

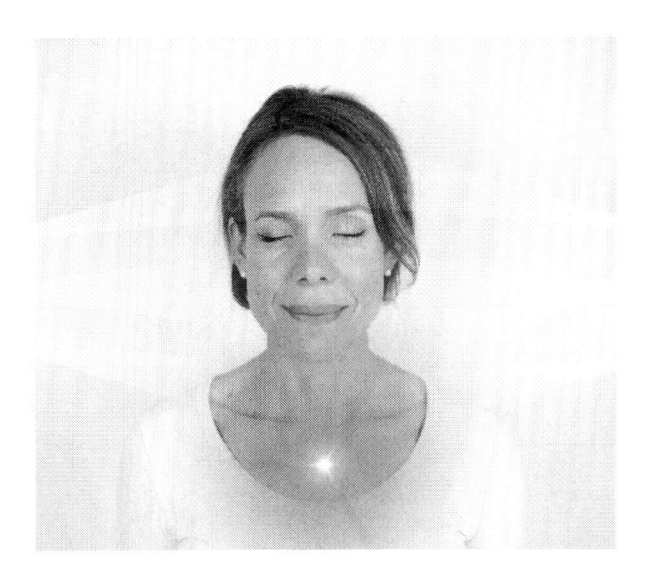

Step #2. Calling in Your Guardian Angel's Light

For many women, asking for and accepting help is a challenge for all of the reasons we have discussed earlier in this book. Becoming comfortable to ask for help or to ask for love is a behaviour that is always rewarded by your guardian angel and is responded to immediately. An essential dynamic of your relationship is asking for help and trusting that it will always be given. Such trust is developed and enhanced through your having repeated evidence of receiving help and love from your guardian angel immediately upon asking.

When we have been disappointed, let down, or betrayed by others in the past, it is natural to want to do things ourselves so we have control over outcomes in our life. Likewise, if love and help have been withheld or conditional in the past, especially if it is because we have not acted in accordance with another's expectations or desires, we learn it is easier to not ask for help. This limiting behaviour, whilst understandable, can keep you from accessing the infinite help and love of your guardian angel.

To counter such difficulties, calling in light is vital to the process of creating the Channel of Clarity between you and your guardian angel. Calling in your guardian angel's light heals conditioned restrictive behaviours and gently and tenderly replaces them with the trust that is built and enjoyed through repeated positive experiences. When you call in your guardian angel's light, it comes instantly, without question, every time. My telling you that it is so is not enough. For that trust to become your truth, you must see evidence of it and experience it for yourself.

Once you develop your heart centre state, the connection with your guardian angel has begun, so calling in your guardian angel's light is a natural progression. This step is vital because it enhances your ability to ask for and accept help, guidance, messages, and answers from your guardian angel.

In the beginning stages, calling in your guardian angel's light is most effective through quiet meditation, but women learn how to do it at work, at home, as they walk, and some like to do it as they shower or bathe. Wherever you are and whatever you ask, your guardian angel is always there for you.

> "When I call you, you come. You don't care how I look, how I am feeling, when it is, how long it has been since the last time I called you. You show up — instantly, every time without question, with exactly the same level of infinite love and help available." Ros speaking of Tressarn.

Hidden Treasures

A byproduct of calling in your guardian angel's light is a feeling of regeneration and rejuvenation of your body. You feel radiant, younger, healthier, and more vital. It is beautiful to witness the appearance of women I mentor change as they become charged with their guardian angel's light. The people in their lives often ask if they have changed their skin cream or been on a health kick. It is a point when many women choose to focus on their health and wellbeing. Some women find they naturally shed unwanted weight they have been carrying for many years, a physical representation of feeling unsupported and alone in life despite having a deeply loving family.

Step #3. Becoming Charged with Your Guardian Angel's Light

This is one of my favourite stages, simply because it makes living your life purpose so clear. You experience the elixir of your life purpose and have everything that you require to live it — your unique strengths. The women I personally mentor discover their unique strengths immediately when I facilitate their connection with their guardian angel. Your guardian angel is your life purpose code, and his or her unique colours hold the precise meaning of each of your unique strengths.

As we discussed earlier in this book, many women are acutely aware of their self-perceived shortcomings, weaknesses, and the things they tell themselves and others they don't do well. For many women, the moment of discovering their unique strengths through their guardian angel is a complete game changer. It is a moment of self-realisation that allows them to see and know themselves in the most powerful and positive way imaginable. They often tell me that they feel truly seen for the first time in their lives. There is a deep acceptance and experience of love that awakens beautiful personal power from within. **When you know your unique strengths, you know yourself in a way that validates the best of what you always hoped to be true about yourself.** Knowing your unique strengths fills you with knowing *I knew I was here for more than this*, and the capability to follow your life purpose path without any doubt or question. Knowing your unique strengths and becoming charged with your guardian angel's light enhance and amplify your most empowering qualities and traits and align you with your true life purpose. These are the ingredients, but there is more to the recipe.

Earlier I stated that knowledge alone is not power. Knowledge applied is power. Once you know your strengths, you must understand how best to use and apply them to your life. When you do, you truly become your strengths. When you are charged with your guardian angel's light, you optimise all of your unique strengths and increase the power of everything you have come to be. You are aligned with your life purpose.

It is the final stage of creating your Channel of Clarity that provides the direct line of communication between you and your guardian angel that guides you to live your true life purpose.

Hidden Treasures

One of the hidden treasures of becoming charged with the light of your guardian angel is self-acceptance. So many women, myself included, have felt for much of their lives that they needed to be something more or something different to be accepted by others. The self-acceptance born from becoming charged with your guardian angel's light, which reflects your unique strengths, creates a deep sense of knowing yourself and being fully comfortable in your own skin. **Women report feeling capable, empowered and fully supported to embrace life in the most positive ways.**

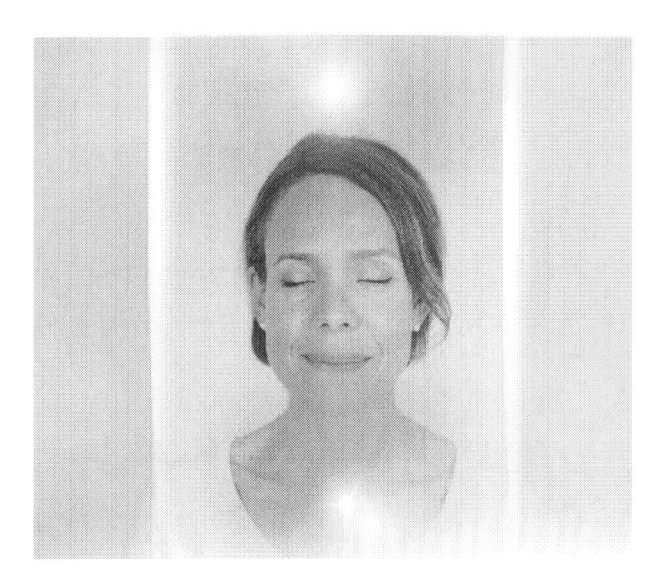

Step #4. Creating Your Channel of Clarity

This is, without a doubt, the least utilized part in all of life purpose discovery. Traditionally, establishing a clear channel of communication between you and your guardian angel was entirely overlooked in favour of waiting for some kind of sign to arrive. Instead, imagine spending time connecting with your guardian angel, asking for help and then having a reliable way of communicating or receiving guidance.

When you create your Channel of Clarity you establish an exceptional direct line of communication that is the life-enhancing conduit through which you see, hear, feel, and know all communication from your guardian angel. To reiterate, through your Channel of Clarity, you receive clear answers and clear life purpose guidance without delays and frustration. From your guardian angel, you receive support and guidance that is enhanced by easier, more efficient, and more effective communication. You can even receive guidance about questions you would not have thought to ask.

You can see that your channel of clarity is a direct line for personal communication between you and your guardian angel.

Often, my clients ask me to help them create their channel of clarity so they can accomplish specific life purpose goals that they have hoped to make a reality for many years. I help clients do that by asking immediate goal-oriented questions and receiving answers and direction straight away.

The creation of your Channel of Clarity is important to get right for two main reasons. First, it is fundamental to the success of your life-changing relationship with your guardian angel. Second, it is essential for gaining the clear guidance and direction you need so you can move forward in the best way, to live your true purpose in life.

Key Chapter Takeaways

The Channel of Clarity between you and your guardian angel can be created with a simple four-step process:

1. **Heart Centre State**
   - The heart centre state is the first step to creating your Channel of Clarity and living your true life purpose. Your heart centre state creates a connection with your guardian angel that becomes more familiar, more natural, stronger, and more developed each time.

2. **Calling in Your Guardian Angel's Light**
   - Calling in your guardian angel's light is one of the most misunderstood and overlooked areas of finding your life purpose path. It is vital as it creates your ability to ask for and accept help, guidance, messages, and answers from your guardian angel.

3. **Becoming Charged with Light**
   - Charged with your guardian angel's light, you optimise all of your unique strengths. You increase the most empowering qualities and traits that align you with your life purpose.

4. **Creating Your Channel of Clarity**
   - Your Channel of Clarity establishes an exceptional direct line of communication between you and your guardian angel. You will receive life-enhancing communication, which you can see, hear, feel and know, from your guardian angel.

Chapter 8

How to Have Meaningful and Productive Conversations with Your Guardian Angel

Find the courage to ask questions and to express what you really want.
-Don Miguel Ruiz

We have just explored the **Channel of Clarity** and we've talked about the importance of the vital steps required to make the **Celestial Formula** work for you. If you were to follow only what I've taught you in this book so far, you'd know how to have a relationship with your guardian angel, which means you can walk along your life purpose path together.

That is only one part of what makes **Channel of Clarity** so effective. Yes, of course, I want you to find and follow your life purpose path but, more than that, I want your communication with your guardian angel to be overflowing with life purpose guidance that creates an ever-enhancing experience of living your life.

In this section, we're going to be discussing the three components needed to experience meaningful and productive conversations with your guardian angel:

1. expectation;

2. good questions; and

3. quieting your mind.

When my clients have all three of these pieces dialed in, they find it effortless to live true life purpose and do so in even more life-enhancing ways.

Let's examine each individually to see exactly how they contribute to the quality of the conversations.

#1. Expectation

A big potential barrier to having meaningful and productive conversations with your guardian angel is your mindset. The expectations you have about conversations with your guardian angel has a huge bearing on how you build your communication. A shift in your mindset is often required for you to communicate clearly and to open yourself fully to receiving the life purpose guidance your guardian angel is waiting to deliver.

You may have noticed that the way you expect a conversation to go has a huge bearing on how it actually goes. Clients are surprised that communication with their guardian angel requires an entire shift in the expectation of what a relationship or even what a conversation can truly be.

For many years, my limiting expectations about relationships restricted my ability to communicate my needs. Fear of rejection caused me to hold back from asking for help. I felt unsupported in my early life and denied help at times when I felt vulnerable and in need, because I learned that when I did ask for help, it was rejected — I was rejected. The result was that, as an adult, I went to great lengths not to ask for help. For many years this affected my relationship with Tressarn, because I blocked his full capacity to help me.

At the very beginning of your relationship with your guardian angel, any reluctance to ask for help, expectations of rejection, or beliefe that you will not be helped restrict your ability both to ask for and to receive communication.

Your guardian angel always helps you, always guides you, always answers your questions, and always supports you to accomplish your life purpose path. They'll prove this to you consistently in ways that rebuild your trust in yourself and provide constant evidence of their unconditional love for you. The relationship with your guardian angel is unlike any other you are likely to have experienced in your lifetime.

Your expectation and anticipation of your guardian angel's help is what allows you to begin meaningful conversations. When you ask a question, an answer is always sent. Every time. Without exception.

Your expectation creates the openness required for conversations with your guardian angel. To begin with, your expectation creates natural, gentle, and subtle communication. The more you expect from and anticipate in your communication, the more you will receive, and the more your meaningful conversations are enhanced and amplified.

The starting place for meaningful conversations with your guardian angel is positive expectation and anticipation of communication.

#2. Good Questions

An important component of meaningful conversations with your guardian angel is your ability to ask really good questions. Your guardian angel's answers can only be as good as the questions you ask. Why is this important? Because the clearer your questions, the better your guardian angel can deliver the answers and clear life purpose guidance directly to you.

Many people fail to make progress in their life purpose by ignoring this simple principle. Closed questions that prompt Yes or No answers severely limit the help you can receive from your guardian angel.

For example, consider the limitation of this question: "Will I win the lottery today?" A good question is focused on what you *really* want. In the case of "Will I win the lottery today?" consider what you *really* want. Do you really want financial security? Perhaps, you really want choice and freedom in your life. You may really want to feel loved and special. Think this through with me.

Unless you ask for what you really want, how can your guardian angel help you get it? Your life purpose is a lifetime of doing the things you love and want to do. You can ask your guardian angel good questions when you know what you want. You vocalise it. Then, together, you and your guardian angel can go get what you want.

With the Channel of Clarity method we've been talking about so far, asking the right questions is an important tool you can use to begin your meaningful and productive conversations with your guardian angel.

Now, we need to determine the following: What kind of questions do we ask? How often do we ask them? And what is the exact structure of those questions? Let's explore question types, frequency, and structure.

#2a. How can we? or What can we do?

The purposes of the "How can we?" or "What can we do? " questions are to foster a relationship of trust and clear communication and to assure you that you and your guardian angel are working together. Only with a relationship of trust and collaboration can you and your guardian angel cocreate your life purpose. Trust is grown through unconditional support and consistent evidence of results.

There are two things that your guardian angel can do to help you trust:

1. prove to you that when you ask for help — they do help; and

2. show you results, so you know you are doing this together.

Questions that begin with "How can we?" or "What can we do?" accomplish a few different things and effectively move you to your true purpose in life. First, a good "How can we?" or "What can we do? " question encourages regular communication with your guardian angel. Asking this kind of question every day is powerful:

How can we (insert what you really want)?

Or

What can we do to (insert what you really want)?

I've found, the more honest and clear you are about what you really want in these questions, the more likely they will do exactly what they're meant to do, produce results. Seeing the results that appear in your life confirms that your guardian angel is helping you. Through this, they nurture your relationship of trust and you know that you are doing this together.

The operative word in this question format is **we**. By its simple insertion, that word creates, through implication, an instant connection and feeling of support and help. From this, you realise and acknowledge you are not alone, you have a relationship with your guardian angel and you are cocreating your life. This makes you an important part of the process. With your questions you create the expectation of what you want, which directs your guardian angel to guide you towards the end result, the essence, and support you in its achievement.

I could go on, but I hope you get the picture. The idea here is to ask your guardian angel good questions so they can give you their best help, in all instances and especially where you might have struggled on blindly and alone in the past.

You see, by asking good, honest, and clear questions you can receive great, authentic, and accurate answers that bring positive results into your life.

#2b. How Often Do You Ask Questions?

Implicit in how often is how many. As I said earlier, there is no limit to number or frequency of the questions you can ask your guardian angel, and you have your entire life to ask them. I find it incredibly clarifying and productive to ask one good question per day; however, only you can say what works best for you.

Ask one good question per day

For those who find it hard to ask for help, a daily question creates a rhythm and consistency that makes asking easier while keeping the guidance coming. Asking one question every day, helps hone your question composing skills, gives you more time to develop clear questions, and allows time for your guardian angel's answers to be applied to your life.

Once you find your question rhythm, the next step is to start working on your ability to hear your guardian angel's answers so you can focus on applying their clear guidance for the best results.

An effective tool for purposeful conversations with your guardian angel is creating a good question, so your guardian angel can give you clear and accurate life purpose guidance.

#3. Quieting Your Mind

A reality many struggle with is clearly hearing their guardian angel's answer and guidance. I hope I can help you overcome such a struggle in this section by helping you quiet your mind.

Few of us actively listen. Often, in our conversations, one person is speaking and many others are waiting to speak. We miss a lot of information and understanding in doing so. Some of us might believe ourselves to be good listeners — but are we actively listening so we can truly hear?

Listening well requires quieting our mind and becoming present to the other people in the conversation. Relentless mind chatter can be distracting. When our minds are full of chatter, the noise can take up all the space. Observe yourself in your next conversation and notice how present or not you are to the person you are with. Are you focused on what they are saying or is your mind wandering off into internal chatter about what's for dinner or whether you fed the cat this morning.

New science in brain imaging lets us watch what happens when we quieten our minds. For many years it was believed that the activity of the brain only changed during the periods when you quietened your mind. But now, multiple studies have shown that the structure of the brain itself can permanently change in a process known as neuralplasticity. When you quieten your mind and enter a meditative state, networks in the brain become activated as if they are glowing and humming with renewed life. As they do so, unhappiness, anxiety, stress, and head noise begin to dissolve, leaving a profound sense of reinvigoration. You feel calm, peaceful, and present and a quiet space is created inside of your head.

Being able to quiet your mind is an important and enjoyable aspect of communicating with your guardian angel. When you ask a good question and then quieten your mind to hear the answer, the answer in your mind rises clearly amidst the source of answers to every single life purpose question. This brings you into a whole new level of living your life purpose. Your communication with your guardian angel has developed to the extent that they can provide you with guidance beyond what you thought to ask. This is living your life purpose at its highest level.

Quieting your mind is vital to hear what your guardian angel so dearly wants you to know. For this reason, meditations with your guardian angel are at the very heart of our program.

When you are able to listen so that you can hear your guardian angel's guidance, you are able to live your life purpose at the highest level possible.

Key Chapter Takeaways

There are three things needed to have meaningful and productive conversations with your guardian angel:

1. **Expectation**
   - The biggest potential barrier to having meaningful and productive conversations with your guardian angel is your mindset. Positive expectations create the best conversations and communication.

2. **Good Questions**
   - The best way to have meaningful and productive conversations with your guardian angel is to ask really good questions. The better your questions, the better the answers you will receive.

3. **Quieting Your Mind**
   - When you quieten your mind to hear your guardian angel's answers, you step into a whole new level of living your life purpose because your guardian angel can provide guidance that you would never have thought to ask for.

Ros Place

Part 3

Getting to Know Your Guardian Angel

Chapter 9

The First Step for Connecting with Your Guardian Angel

"I've learned that whenever I decide to do something with an open heart, I usually make the right decision."
– Maya Angelou

Uncertainty of who their guardian angel is has kept many people from using their **Channel of Clarity** to find and follow their life purpose. Unfortunately, in our society we have created a barrier between us and our guardian angels. Most people are convinced that the only true reality is that which can be seen and accepted by all. Yet, we were all born with a guardian angel by our side. Many of us felt or knew their presence in some way as a child. The child smiling and laughing in their crib, when no one can be seen, knows their guardian angel. The wisdom seen in a newborn baby's eyes reflects they know their guardian angel. The struggle of the physical world and the conditioning we experience as we grow, causes the connection with your guardian angel to fade a little more with each day of our physical existence.

Connecting with your guardian angel is something you may have wanted to do without realising. The desire shows up in subtle ways. It can be a feeling that something is missing, when you seem to have so much and are grateful for what you have. It can be a feeling that you are here for something more, even though you don't know what that more could possibly be. It could be a yearning inside of you to live the life you just can't put your finger on but know you really came here to live. Then, again, you may have consciously wanted to connect, but didn't know how or where to go to find out.

To truly connect, you must be willing to approach life in a new way that allows your guardian angel to show you your strengths and the highest version of yourself, so you can live the life for which you came. You also must be willing to commit to finding and following your life purpose path with your guardian angel by your side. With unconditional love, they guide and support us every step of the way.

What your connection with your guardian angel does better than mentoring, coaching, or therapy routes is to deliver information to you — in a way that you can instantly trust. Validating your thoughts, feelings, and choices for yourself, helps your connection be and feel secure.

It should be noted that though it may feel like you are trying to *meet* your guardian angel, they are already with you all the time, and have been since you were conceived. Until you take steps to *connect* with them, truly knowing your guardian angel is almost impossible. It happens when you open your heart and ask *"Dear Guardian Angel, how can I connect with you so I can live my true purpose in life?"* Truly connecting with them can take work; likely, much more than just one afternoon .

A connection with your guardian angel is nonlinear. It's organic. It may come to you in the shower, in dreams, when you find time to be still and quiet — probably not while staring at your computer. Going on walks, journaling about it, feeling more love in your heart, and starting to feel trust grow are ways you can develop your ability to connect with them. So, remember, this is a process.

You might use all, some, or none of the instructions I'm about to give you to connect with your guardian angel. You might just be one of the lucky ones who wakes up one day and the connection between you is established and ready to go. If that's you, embrace it and run with the life purpose guidance your connection with your guardian angel provides, and as directly as your connection allows.

When working with a client, I often spend a week leading up to their guardian angel connection session, just getting to know their guardian angel. I open the channels of communication with their guardian angel and sometimes the guardian angel provides their name first and other times they show themselves and their colours to me first. Sometimes a guardian angel wants me to feel their human's strengths, and sometimes they speak to me and tell me what it is they want me to know.

I prefer to take my time to get to know your guardian angel and I encourage you to do the same. It is a sacred partnership and, whatever your age is, that is the number of years you and they have to catch up.

Keep that in mind when you start developing your connection with your guardian angel and be patient. If you don't get it right away, you are still on the right track. You do best if you stay ready, keep yourself open, maintain your expectation, keep playing, and experimenting.

When you connect, it sticks to you like a revelation. You won't be able to shake the bliss and right away, you start seeing positive changes appearing everywhere in your life, kind of like when you see the first spring blossom and soon blossoms are everywhere. Once you start intentionally living your life purpose, life gets very exciting.

Key Chapter Takeaways

- To find and follow your life purpose path you need to connect with your guardian angel.

- The first step to connecting with your guardian angel is to open yourself to meeting them.

- Once you master the skill of connecting with your guardian angel, you have all you ever need to live your true life purpose.

Ros Place

Chapter 10

Three Core Elements all Guardian Angels Have in Common

"We accept the love we think we deserve"
– Stephen Chbosky

Over the past 18 years, I've connected hundreds of women with their guardian angels and, in that time, I've seen three common core elements in all guardian angels: a unique name, a special number, and they share their person's unique life purpose strengths. Understand these, and your guardian angel acts as an incredible guide to living your true purpose in life. Ignore these elements, and you have a hard time moving forwards along your life purpose path.

#1. Your Guardian Angel Has A Unique Name

Tressarn

That's my guardian angel's name. I never knew his name until I asked him to tell me what it was. As a child, I always knew it was him by the way he felt and made me feel. A name was not something I even thought of, until someone asked me what my guardian angel's name was. Only, when I was asked that, I realised I didn't know what it was because it was not something I had ever used. It's an unusual name — not a name or word I'd heard before — it is unique as is he, as are we all. At first it felt odd to use because I had never called him by name before. It is a beautiful name and it means "Inspirational Encourager". His name describes part of my life purpose path, which makes complete sense to me. I've always loved to encourage people and help them to feel inspired to live their best life possible.

My husband's guardian angel is called Prega. Her name means "Appreciated Wisdom", which is part of his life purpose, and when Eddie learned Prega's name and its meaning, he said it made complete sense to him, too. In our house we call Eddie, The Bringer of Information. He loves to research and find out about things — often along a path less travelled. The information that Eddie brings into our lives, on everything from natural remedies to his ability to think outside of the box and solve problems, are all much appreciated wisdom.

Your guardian angel's name is completely unique and its meaning ties in with your unique life purpose. **Knowing your guardian angel's name immediately provides a concise and significant message about your life purpose.**

You may have noticed that I referred to Tressarn as he and Prega as she. Guardian angels do not have a gender. They are not, nor ever have been, male or female. They are energy and have never held a physical form.

What I am sharing with you here, is the first of the three common elements. Your guardian angel's name carries a tiny piece of your life purpose and provides you with an instant connection and a highly significant validation of who they are and by connection, who you are. It is something that is simple and memorable — your guardian angel's name.

#2. Your Guardian Angel Has a Special Number

Your guardian angel's special number is not unique, but has important significance. It is within the range from four to eight, and relates to an over-arching character theme of your life purpose. Your guardian angel's special number is shown as their number of bands. I have, as yet, only ever encountered two individuals whose guardian angel number is four. One of them is guardian angel to an American billionaire who asked me to connect him with his guardian angel, which I did when I was visiting Los Angeles. The second is a vice-president at a large record label. Both individuals are laser-focused on their career and have accomplished remarkable outcomes in their pure purpose of work, business, and career. Similarly, I have met only one guardian angel with eight as their special number. This particular guardian angel belonged to an almost teenage girl at the time. Guardian angels with eight as their special number are focused on bringing harmony to the earth. I have a feeling more eights will be found in the younger generations to come. Fives and sixes are most common, with the occasional seven.

Tressarn is a five and his bands reflect my overarching life purpose theme, which relates to freedom and choice. Prega is a six, which reflects Eddie's purpose of helping others in ways that also support his growth and wellbeing. And finally, the occasional sevens are a rare breed of individuals, who hunger to explore ideas and go on constant adventures.

Which of these sounds most like you?

Here are descriptions of the guardian angel special numbers:

Fours are pure work and business focused individuals who are laser focussed on making ideas reality and building empires.

Fives are freedom-seeking lovers of change who love to motivate and inspire others to get the most from their lives.

Sixes are supportive and empowering champions of others who naturally give themselves to helping others.

Sevens are entranced by the journey of discovery, research and exploration who love to go on adventures in life.

Eights are true harmony creators who naturally seek to unify, bring together and provide space for alternative perspectives to be heard.

3. Your Guardian Angel Shares Your Unique Life Purpose Strengths

The last common element is that your guardian angel shares your unique life purpose strengths. You may wonder how strengths can be unique and shared. As mentioned earlier, your guardian angel is with you, only you, from the moment of conception. In a sense, you are a combined unit, from that time on and throughout this present physical experience. You were born with certain strengths that are integral to your unique purpose, your unique guardian angel, and your unique experience of life. By sharing these strengths, your guardian angel can help you discover and develop them so that you can find and follow your life purpose path in the easiest and most direct way. Finding and developing your strengths is a simple but powerful step that is done more easily than you might expect. Being willing to open yourself up and then working with your guardian angel to develop those strengths are valuable and enjoyable endeavours that lead to living your unique life purpose fully. So, why are your strengths unique?

Even if you believe that you are basically the same as everyone else, your strengths, your capabilities, your natural talents, and the way you approach life — to say nothing of all that you have learned and experienced — means it's impossible for anyone to be exactly like you or for you to be exactly like them. A large number of women clients don't recognize or understand what their special qualities and strengths are and have taken little time to sit down and think about themselves in that way. Instead, many have spent more time trying to fix their shortcomings rather than develop their strengths. All too often, women struggle through their whole life with their unique strengths untapped.

You only find your true purpose in life by doing what you love to do and are good at doing. The key is identifying the unique life purpose strengths you were born with and understanding precisely how to apply them to your life. This is done by getting to know your guardian angel and your unique life purpose strengths. As you connect with your guardian angel, no matter how new and blossoming the connection seems right now, this source of life purpose communication improves over time. And, while you are improving your connection with your guardian angel, you also are living your true purpose and doing what you love to do. **Your connection with your guardian angel is how you tap into your unique strengths and, together, have the best possible life imaginable.**

Later in this book I'll be giving you the opportunity to explore your unique life purpose strengths and **identify your top three life purpose strength areas.**

Putting it all Together

Understand the three core elements all guardian angels have in common and that your guardian angel acts as an incredible guide to living your true purpose in life. Ignore these elements, as I've said before, and you'll have a hard time moving forwards along your life purpose path.

Getting all three core elements may take some effort. I won't sugar coat it. You'll need to be willing to open yourself to new things. However, if you're willing to put in the effort, to do what many others don't, you'll be able to live the life that others can't. You'll experience life as a woman who has done the work and is set to live her life purpose with true success.

I can promise you this: if you connect with your guardian angel, you'll be amazed at the ripple effect it has in your life, and on the lives of those who you love and care about. Trust me when I say it's worth the effort to do and get it right.

As you've been following along so far in this book, you've done something—a few somethings. You've analysed your current life situation in the beginning chapters, and you've learned **The Celestial Formula** and how it fits into creating your **Channel of Clarity** with your guardian angel. By the end of this book, you'll have started connecting with your guardian angel, maybe you'll have reached out for help, identified your top three life purpose strengths, and are well on the way to finding your purpose in life with your guardian angel.

Key Chapter Takeaways

- All Guardian Angels have the same three core elements:

- **#1. Your Guardian Angel Has a Unique Name**
  Your guardian angel's name is completely unique with a unique life purpose meaning.

- **#2. Your Guardian Angel Has a Special Number**
  Your guardian angel's number can be any number between 4 and 8 and it relates to an over-arching character theme of your life purpose. Rarest are 4s and 8s; the majority of us have 5 or 6.

- **#3. Your Guardian Angel Shares Your Unique Life Purpose Strengths**
  You have special qualities that are unique to you. Even if you believe that you are the same as everyone else, you have strengths, capabilities, and natural talents that only you have and which are reflected in your guardian angel's bands.

Chapter 11

How to Connect with Your Guardian Angel

"You will never plough a field if you only turn it over in your mind."
– Irish Proverb

If you've made it to this chapter, then you have a good understanding of how your guardian angel can provide you with clear life purpose guidance through your channel of clarity. You should also, by now, have a few ideas about how your guardian angel can help you to live your true life purpose, and you are ready for the connection process.

There is something I want to say before we dive too deeply into the process of connecting with your guardian angel. The first step to connecting is love. Love. Sounds so simple, right? Connection with your guardian angel is developed as you allow more love. Each time you connect you take a small step towards allowing more of their love to reach you. This stage cannot be rushed, forced, or pushed. You must learn to not try to make it happen. Instead, you must learn to allow. **Your connection with your guardian angel is how you allow their love to reach you.**

Step 1 — Set a time for your guardian angel connection and honour it

The hardest part of making a connection with your guardian angel is getting started. The second hardest part is doing it all again tomorrow. This is evidenced by the following pattern that commonly occurs with a person's initial attempts to connect with their guardian angel:

> Day 1: Filled with excitement, they sit down in their comfy chair, quieten their mind and enjoy a feeling of stillness for 10 minutes. They feel lighter, they are enjoying the process, and they agree to be patient and take their time — they are beginning the process.

> Day 2: They sit back down in their comfy chair. They reflect on what they felt the day before and start questioning themselves, *"Am I doing it right? Am I really capable of connecting with my guardian angel?"* They sit for 5 minutes and try to quieten their mind — many of those minutes are interrupted by thoughts about how they should be feeling and if and when the connection will happen. The lightness and stillness from yesterday isn't coming. It's not as much fun anymore.

> Day 3: They think, *"Maybe I need a break. I'll try again tomorrow."* Self-doubt starts to grow and take over. It's a struggle to quieten their mind and their inability to find any stillness fuels excuses for not trying today.

Day 4 through Day 30: These days are filled with starts and stops, huffing and starting over, sitting in a different chair, trying to make it happen, spending time analysing and thinking about all the reasons why they are the one person on earth who can't do it, and eventually chasing Shiny Object Syndrome and jumping to a new tactic entirely.

Months later, they see the words "guardian angel" (it's amazing how often those two words pop up in daily life) in an article, on the TV, or as they walk into a store. They remember about connecting with their guardian angel and that they could be living their life purpose, which it definitely feels they aren't. Kicking themselves, they say, *"This time I'm gonna make it work!"* and the cycle starts all over.

So, how do you get off that destructive loop? How do you prevent yourself from ever getting there in the first place?

1. Build the skill of connecting with your guardian angel.

Realise that connecting with your guardian angel is accomplished in the same manner as all new worthwhile skills. Developed over time, they are challenging at the beginning, uncomfortable, inconvenient, but the effort of developing them is expansive and totally worth it.

Most of the women who quit before they have created a connection with their guardian angels do so because they thought the connection was going to be instant. When it isn't, they bail, thinking something was wrong with them, their ability, or the process. Nothing is wrong. That's just the nature of developing a beautiful new skill.

> Don't get me wrong, there are so many beautiful, fun, exciting and massively rewarding parts to creating your connection with your guardian angel. The key, I've found, is to enter into the process with a heart and mind open to learning something new and magnificent that will transform your entire life.

Tressarn talks about connection as a learned technique, similar to driving. To begin with, learning to drive feels like an extremely complicated and confusing process. It's all totally new and you need to do lots of things at the same time. You wonder if you'll ever get there! Yet, you see hundreds of people driving cars every day. So, you know you just have to practise and you'll learn. But after dedicating time to learning to drive, you get your driver's licence and you can drive without instruction. After a time, you even find yourself driving from A to B and the process has become so automatic you can't remember how you got there. During that time, you are not doubting that it is possible to drive. Just because you can't see hundreds of people connecting and channelling every day, don't doubt it is happening. I promise you, it is happening and it's happening for hundreds, maybe thousands, of women every single day. Likely, most of those women were once at the very beginning, wondering just like you if they'd ever learn to drive.

2. Time block your connection time with your guardian angel.

> Like a job, have a set time for connecting with your guardian angel. I don't recommend chunking out more than 15 minutes at first. Connecting with your guardian angel is like exercising a muscle. Think of it as training for a marathon. If you started your first day of training with a 4-hour run, you wouldn't be

able to walk the next day. As a result, you'd quit your training.

The same goes for connecting with your guardian angel. Start slow, start small, and build up. It won't take weeks, probably only a few days, and you'll be able to go on and on, connecting with your guardian angel more quickly and using the rest of the time to communicate about your life purpose.

3. Keep a journal to track your connection time.

    What is measured can be improved. Getting an accurate measure of your progress is a good way to self-motivate. Knowing that your connection with your guardian angel develops further each time you allow yourself to connect, can support your success. If there are any small exceptions to the time you have promised yourself, understanding how the process compounds your ability can help motivate you to manage yourself and make up for those missed days.

    I recommend using a journal or a diary to track your guardian angel connection time. Seeing how consistent you have been, also contributes to your self-motivation to continue building your skill of connecting.

4. Celebrate your progress.

    I think we spend a lot of time in society today celebrating non-achievement and ignoring our own actual achievement, to our detriment. There is a universal law, called the *Law of Increase*, that says whatever you give your attention to, will flourish and grow. Giving your attention to the small, lovely experiences you have acknowledges and celebrates those experiences. Celebrate connecting for seven days straight. Celebrate feeling more familiarity with connecting with your guardian angel. Celebrate any subtle feelings of increased love. Celebrate the peace the connection time brings.

When you have created your connection with your guardian angel, do something special and train your brain that setting goals and accomplishing them feels really, really good.

Connecting with your guardian angel is learning a life-changing and worthwhile skill. Put in the time, show up every day and, sooner than you think, you'll have created a connection with your guardian angel. Through that connection, you can receive all of the life purpose guidance you need to live the life you came here to live.

Step 2 - Allow Your Guardian Angel's Love to Reach You

Maybe for the first time ever, you have a chance to feel the love of your guardian angel. It's a love like no other you will ever experience in your life. It's difficult to imagine or explain the unconditional, continuous, and infinite nature of the love that your guardian angel has for you as you are right now.

Earlier in the chapter, I explained that the first step to connecting with your guardian angel is love. It sounds and is simple. The way to connect with your guardian angel is to learn to open your heart centre and welcome their love.

The more love you can allow, the more your connection blossoms and grows.

Tressarn uses lots of different words to describe allowing. He says it is a natural process that develops over time and is always on your terms. Tressarn explains that allowing starts with giving your guardian angel permission to love you, then it happens gently and tenderly — no pushing, no rushing, no persuading, no convincing. Allowing your guardian angel's love to reach you happens on your terms, in your way. You're in the driver's seat, so to speak, and the gentle, tender, and consistent love you receive from your guardian angel nurtures your ability to allow more and more of their love to reach you.

So, let your guardian angel love you as they find you. There is no need for striving for perfection of any kind. There is no requirement to be different, better, or more in any way.

One goal of your connection with your guardian angel is to allow their love to reach you.

I've spent some time with Tressarn to create a special step-by-step meditation script for you to help you connect with your guardian angel by learning to gently and tenderly allow more of their love to reach you.

Feeling the Love of Your Guardian Angel

You might like to ask a friend or loved one to read these words to you. You might like to read the words yourself or even record yourself speaking these words out loud.

This meditation has been created to help you to feel the love of your guardian angel. The more love you can feel from your guardian angel, the more connected you become. The more connected you become, the more your guardian angel can guide you to live your true life purpose.

Your guardian angel is with you now, helping and loving you.

You can ask to feel your guardian angel's love every day and develop a connection between you.

Your guardian angel is with you now and helping and loving you.

1. Close your eyes and adjust your posture so that you are comfortable. Place your hands in your lap and, if it is comfortable, have your palms facing upwards. Imagine your whole body relaxing, starting with your toes. Bring that feeling of relaxation into your feet, your calves, your thighs. Continue to bring a feeling of relaxation into your abdomen and lower back, your chest, your upper back and your shoulders. Bring relaxing comfort into your arms, your hands, your neck, your head, and your face.

2. Begin to breathe into your upper chest and lift your chest upwards with a deep breath so your spine is upright. As you do this, you may want to adjust the back of your head and dip your chin slightly to your chest.

3. Imagine, now, that a beautiful shimmering radiant light is shining down upon you. Feel the radiance of the light of pure love. Picture beautiful filaments of pure white, loving light shining upon you. As these filaments of pure, white, loving light touch you, feel your vibration increase.

4. Feel love surrounding you and begin to take in the radiance of this pure, white, loving light. It is the loving light of your guardian angel.

Your guardian angel's loving light is creating a beautiful energy in your body that gently awakens your heart to feel more love. Allow your guardian angel's pure, white, loving light to gently fill your heart with more love.

5. Place your hand over your heart now and say to yourself, with true feeling:

> I love you.
>
> I accept you for all you are.
>
> I love you unconditionally.

Spend a few moments as you say each one, and feel the loving truth of your words resonate within you.

6. Feel the light from your heart increase your feelings of love and raise your vibration. Feel your heart regenerating your body and radiating love and light to every cell in your body. Imagine now that with each breath you take, you are allowing more of your guardian angel's pure white, loving light to reach you. Feel the pure love that is reaching you from your guardian angel. Bask in this feeling in your heart. Feel this beautiful, loving, pure, white light radiate to every single part of you.

7. Give yourself a moment now to enjoy feeling the love of your guardian angel. It's time to come back now. Coming back with your heart full of love. It's time to come back to your body. Take a deep breath and feel the glow of love throughout your whole body.

Thank your guardian angel for always sending their love to you.

Putting It All Together

By following these steps for connecting with your guardian angel, you'll have no problem creating a channel of communication through which you can receive all the life purpose guidance you will ever need. What's more, you'll be living your true purpose in life because you'll be receiving guidance directly from your guardian angel and together you'll find and follow your life purpose path.

All of this is yours if, and only if, you create your connection with your guardian angel. That is step one. The rest only comes once the first has been accomplished. Do whatever you can to create your connection with your guardian angel. I promise, it changes your life.

Key Chapter Takeaways

- The first step to connecting with your guardian angel is love. The more love you allow the stronger your connection becomes.

- Give your guardian angel permission to love you.

- Allowing your guardian angel's love to reach you happens on your terms, in your way.

- The more of your guardian angel's love you allow, the more their love can reach you. As more love reaches you, you create a stronger connection and so the process continues.

Ros Place

Chapter 12

How to Discover Your Unique Life Purpose Strengths

"Nothing is so strong as gentleness, nothing so gentle and loving as real strength."
-Charles Haddon Spurgeon

This chapter is extremely important and holds the key to your success in using this book.

Why?

Because, when you connect with your guardian angel to find and follow your life purpose path, knowing your unique strengths empowers you to live the life you came to live. Connecting with your guardian angel is how you learn what those unique strengths are. That is why connecting with your guardian angel is the key to living your true purpose in life. The unique strengths that your guardian angel reveals provide a clear framework from which to live your true purpose in life.

Earlier in this book, you may remember from my own story, that it is not enough to *know* your life purpose, you must understand how to apply this knowledge to your life so it can be truly lived. Your guardian angel knows all of your unique life purpose strengths and as they reveal them to you, they show you how best to use them in your life. And, your guardian angel guides you every step of the way along your life purpose path.

This is important so I will say it again: **your guardian angel knows all of your unique life purpose strengths and how you can use them to live your true life purpose.**

Knowing your unique life purpose strengths determines two things:

1. the remarkable truth of what your greatest strengths, gifts, and talents are, and with them the amazing potential you have within you; and

2. through your unique strengths you know what your true life purpose is and how your strengths relate to your purpose.

Once you know your strengths, you can focus on doing what you love, doing what you naturally do best, and maximizing the life purpose guidance your guardian angel can provide through your channel of clarity.

Your life purpose strengths reflect all of the things you are good at doing and being. They are the true remarkable you, the you that exists deep inside and that you may have hoped to be on the outside. You can think of your life purpose strengths as your true self, and the true you was born to be happy and fulfilled in life.

The goal of your Channel of Clarity is to experience a two-way communication with your guardian angel so you can ask for and receive guidance. That guidance helps you know exactly how to apply your strengths to your life purpose and supports you to become authentically yourself. Once you understand exactly how to apply your strengths to your life purpose, you and your guardian angel can cocreate a meaningful, purposeful life.

Remember **The Celestial Formula?**

When you Connect, Communicate and Cocreate with your guardian angel, living your life purpose is imminent and guaranteed.

Connect with your guardian angel and discover your life purpose strengths

Communicate with your guardian angel through a two-way communication channel so you can ask for and receive life purpose guidance.

Cocreate together with your guardian angel so you can maximize the ways you can do what you love and easily live your true life purpose.

To recap, your life purpose strengths are completely unique and they are pinpoint specific to you. You may be aware of some of your life purpose strengths and they are validated through the connection with your guardian angel. Some of your life purpose strengths are latent and really nice surprises that make perfect sense once they are revealed.

Channel of Clarity Method

The Nine Core Life Purpose Strengths

Tressarn has helped me create the summary of each of the nine core life purpose strengths for you. Remembering that your unique life purpose strengths are pinpoint specific to you, within each strength there are infinite hues of each colour that relate to all the personal nuances that exist.

Please read through the descriptions of what each of the colours represent below, then fill out each Life Purpose Strength Self Assessment. Your highest three scores are your top three life purpose strengths.

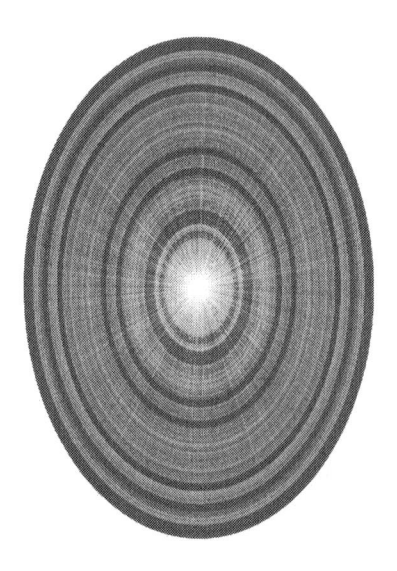

Deep Blue Life Purpose Strength: Courage & Loyalty

Deep blue as a life purpose strength is often present for those of you who have wise souls and loyal hearts. More than that, to have deep blue as a strength means you have the courage and confidence to envision what you know you want in life and the loyalty to yourself to make it your living reality.

Courage

Courage is choosing to do something even when it ventures into a new or unknown territory. It takes courage to do new things and move out of your comfort zone. It is not always easy to face challenging experiences in your life and to take necessary action. Doing so, though, helps you develop confidence in yourselves and in your capabilities so you can act when you feel nervous or fearful. As you see yourself succeeding at doing new things, your inner strength grows. Courage helps you step beyond your limiting comfort zone so you can reach for what you truly desire.

Loyalty

Deep blues signify loyalty and sincerity. Persons who have this colour, stay true to a person or a cause and honour your given word. Loyalty, then, engenders trust in others. Deep blues understand that your word is your bond and you tend to take time before making a commitment. You tend to understand the power of your words and enjoy giving sincere compliments. You naturally see and highlight the most positive attributes of others and tend to show compassion and care with your encouraging manner.

Signs you may have a deep blue life purpose strength:
People tell you that you are strong.
You are self aware.
You like to take people as you find them.
You love to think about your future.

Benefits of having a deep blue strength:
Personal courage
Non-judgemental attitude
Highly capable

Top 10 Deep Blue Life Purpose Themes

Courage

Loyalty

Confidence

Strength

Meditation

Honour

Sincerity

Knowledge

Depth

Envisioning

Find Out if You Have Deep Blue Life Purpose Strength:

Below, rate yourself on a scale from 1—10 on how accurate the statements are—1 means "not accurate at all," and 10 means "most accurate."

Deep Blue Life Purpose Strength Assessment	Self-Rating
I enjoy envisioning my future	
I have vivid dreams	
I like to do new things	
I love to use my imagination	
I am capable of learning new things	
I find it easy to see the good in others	
I am a visual learner	
If I can't imagine something, it doesn't happen	
My word is my bond	
I give sincere compliments	
My Score	

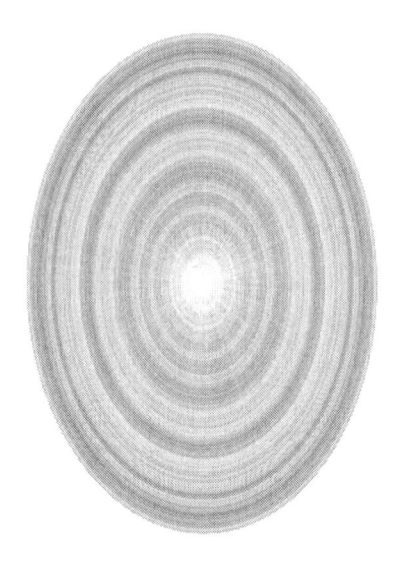

Gold as a Life Purpose Strength: Success & Prosperity

Gold as a life purpose strength indicates an individual's potential for great success. Gold is a strength that often appears to those of you who are enthusiastic and driven to make a difference in the world. Golds often create different versions of success throughout a lifetime, as you come to understand what success really means to you at each stage of your life.

Success

Those with gold as a life purpose strength are here to experience success. Golds find success most easily when you listen to your heart. You understand the importance of defining success for yourself and know that success comes when you live a life rich with purpose and meaning. The mark of true success for golds comes when you look in the mirror and know that you are on your right path. Golds express the valuable contribution you have to make in life and live your life honouring integrity and authenticity, through which you succeed in ways that bring the highest good and in which you thrive the most.

Prosperity

Gold as a strength indicates wealth and many wonderful forms of abundance and prosperity. Golds are born to prosper and thrive. You learn how to acknowledge and appreciate what you have and can easily increase abundance in your life. Golds are sincere in your appreciation and seem to ooze an energy of plenty and growth, always attracting more. Golds always count your blessings and enjoy sharing them with others.

Signs you may have a gold life purpose strength:
People tell you that you inspire them.
You are generous and share with others.
You are fascinated by finding out what makes successful people tick.
You have goals.

Benefits of having a gold strength:
Self-motivation
Enthusiasm and drive to succeed in life
Ease and enjoyment in living abundantly

Top 10 gold life purpose themes

Success

Prosperity

Generosity

Fulfilment

Achievement

Value

Triumph

Choice

Accumulation

Accomplishment

Find Out if You Have a Gold Life Purpose Strength:

Below, rate yourself on a scale from 1—10 on how accurate the statements are—1 means "not accurate at all," and 10 means "most accurate."

Gold Life Purpose Strength Assessment	Self-Rating
I love to explore new ideas and projects	
I am enthusiastic and passionate	
I love the feeling of success	
I enjoy thinking about the things that are working in my life	
I always want to be better today than I was yesterday	
I love seeing others succeed	
I enjoy being around successful people	
I want to be successful in my life	
I don't settle for less than I deserve	
I have my own personal version of success	
My Score	

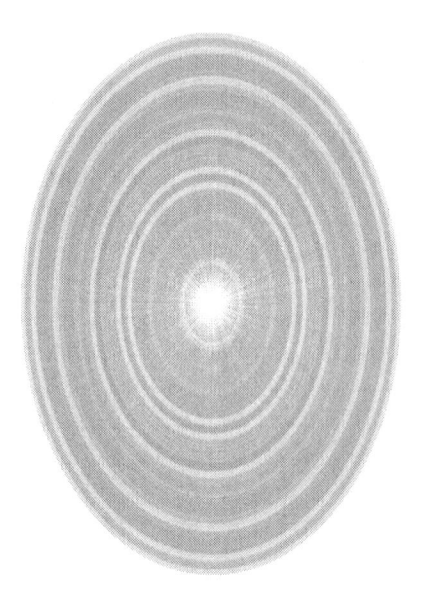

Green as a Life Purpose Strength: Healing & Helping

Green is a life purpose strength that is often present to those of you who are born wanting to help make a difference in the world. To have green as a strength means you have a naturally healing presence that can help others to experience improvement in their lives.

Healing

Those of you with a green life purpose strength are often drawn to explore different ways of bringing healing and wellbeing into the world. Greens can be motivated to learn about healing from a young age and can follow a traditional medical route. You bring healing into others' lives in a multitude of ways. Some greens sense that you are here to make a positive contribution to their local community. Some of you are drawn to spend time outdoors and soak in the healing energy of nature. Others of you feel and sense things that others don't and are gifted with the healing ability of empathy. Many of you healers and bringers of wellbeing have a strong moral inner compass to do good and are guided wisely by your intuition.

Helping

Greens have a strong sense of wanting to offer support. Greens are drawn instinctively to helping others and find it easy to give time and offer support. You all have your own ways of helping others and universally enjoy the feeling of being there as a constant for others. Greens have tremendous empathy and wish to help others, though you yourself may feel unsupported in your own life. The most vibrant and thriving greens create healthy boundaries and prioritise your own wellbeing in order to improve your ability to help others. Greens need more rest and sleep than others as you are powerful tonics that naturally increase wellbeing and enhance your good feelings about life.

Signs you may have a green life purpose strength:

People tell you that you always make them feel better.

You enjoy thinking of ways that you can make things better in the world.

You get a healing glow from spending time in nature.

You love visiting places with good energy.

Benefits of having a green life purpose strength:

Bringer of true improvement

Natural healing and calming presence.

Ability to resolve disputes by helping both parties see their common ground

Top 10 green life purpose themes

Healing

Helping

Health

Wellbeing

Vitality

Regeneration

Improvement

Growth

Evolving

Nurturing

Find Out if You Have a Green Life Purpose Strength

Below, rate yourself on a scale from 1—10 on how accurate the statements are—1 means "not accurate at all," and 10 means "most accurate."

Green Life Purpose Strength Assessment	Self-Rating
I love to make things better for others	
I love to care for others	
I love to do things that I feel can help someone in some way	
I love to send healing energy to others	
I am an empath	
I feel and see things that others do not	
People I have just met often open up and talk to me	
Animals are often drawn to me	
I am drawn towards alternative treatments	
I love to focus on my own wellbeing	
My Score	

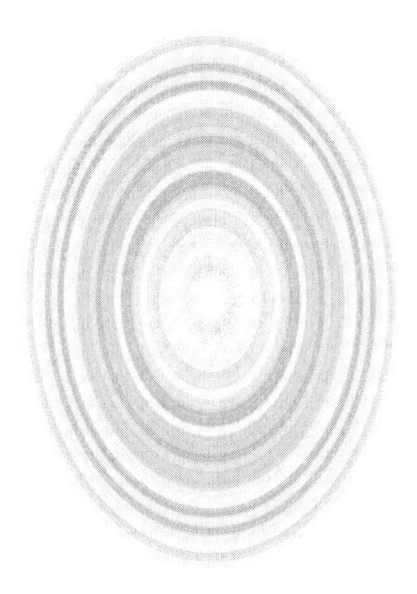

Yellow as a Life Purpose Strength: Optimism & Value

Yellow is a life purpose strength for those of you who are born with a positive outlook on life. Yellows are natural optimists rooted in a deep sense of your own value. Yellows know your own worth, grow belief in themselves, and choose to honour your true value and power.

Optimism

Those of you with yellow life purpose strengths live life with natural optimism. Yellows believe that your life and the outcomes, events and experiences in it, are positive. Yellows see life challenges as temporary setbacks rather than permanent obstacles. Your attitude to conquering life challenges means that you can always easily see the possibility of change and improvement. Yellows tend to look for meaning in adversity and choose to grow through their challenges, which can make you highly resilient.

Value

Yellows learn your value and worth and empower yourselves to create the most positive outcomes in all areas of your life. You value yourselves authentically and by doing so, create a powerful approach to life that leads you to live abundantly. Those of you with a yellow life purpose strength value yourselves, your energy, and your time, and value others in the same way to create positive relationship dynamics. Yellows are constantly expanding into new levels of worthiness, which perpetuate your levels of optimism and create many more things to value and appreciate in life.

Signs you may have a yellow life purpose strength:
People remark on your optimistic attitude.

You love to encourage others.

You look for positive solutions.

You know deep in your heart that belief in yourself is key to creating the life of your dreams.

Benefits of having a yellow life purpose strength:
Positive and close relationships

Optimistic attitude

Personal empowerment

Top 10 yellow life purpose themes
Optimism
Value
Self-belief
Worth
Value
Empowerment
Positivity
Joy
Enlightenment
Bliss

Find Out if You Have a Yellow Life Purpose Strength

Below, rate yourself on a scale from 1—10 on how accurate the statements are—1 means "not accurate at all," and 10 means "most accurate."

Yellow Life Purpose Strength Assessment	Self-Rating
I know that self belief is a vital to success	
I have a positive mental attitude	
I believe in the the power of my thoughts	
I have positive expectations	
I understand the value of appreciation	
I am appreciative	
I value the little things in life	
I love to encourage others	
I see potential in others	
I believe that positive expectations create positive outcomes	
My Score	

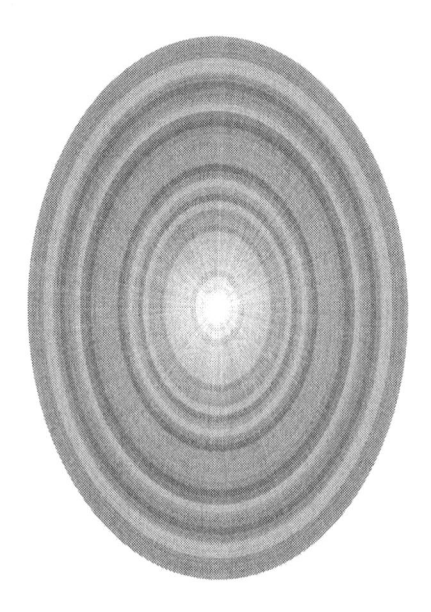

Pink as a Life Purpose Strength: Empathy & Compassion

Pink is a life purpose strength to those of you who are sensitive, with developed emotional intelligence and sensitivity. Pinks are compassionate individuals, who bring a level of care to situations that makes others feel valued, respected, and appreciated and you inspire others to open to their true potential.

Empathy

Empathy is a strong theme for those of you with a pink life purpose strength and this can create a strong calling to help others and make a difference in the world. Pinks have an innate sense of when situations need to be addressed and instinctively know how to bring out the best in others in order to create the best results. You know how to make people feel understood, valued, respected and appreciated — and encourage people to become more open. Pinks learn to empower others by learning to accept and appreciate yourselves first and grow self-trust through your high emotional intelligence. Pinks learn to empower yourselves and others with empathy and your understanding of challenges in life. Your personal journey becomes an important part of the way you can truly empower others.

Compassion

Pinks with the life purpose strength of compassion possess a powerful leadership quality. Pinks are able to help others feel that they matter and to understand how their contribution counts. To feel valuable is one of the most important catalysts of growth. There is a strong correlation between the care demonstrated by compassion and the inspiration of others to perform at your highest level. Treating people with compassion makes people feel they matter, know why they matter, and what they contribute. Pinks have highly developed leadership skills that are focussed on bringing out the best in others and showing a care for the people around you.

Signs you may have a pink life purpose strength:

People tell you that you are caring.

You enjoy helping others and supporting them through challenging situations.

You get a warm feeling inside when you see good people in the world.

You enjoy being kind to others.

Benefits of having a pink strength:
Emotional intelligence
Gentle and compassionate handling of difficult situations
Ability to bring out the best in others

Top 10 pink life purpose themes
Empathy
Compassion
Generosity
Receiving
Acceptance
Abundance
Kindness
Openness
Sensitivity
Trustworthiness

Find Out if You Have Pink as a Life Purpose Strength

Below, rate yourself on a scale from 1—10 on how accurate the statements are—1 means "not accurate at all," and 10 means "most accurate."

Pink Life Purpose Strength Assessment	Self-Rating
I love to encourage others to develop their potential	
I am positive and optimistic	
I love to feel I can make a difference in the world	
I love to give and receive love	
I love seeing others succeed and thrive	
I believe in abundance	
I believe my path is important	
I expect the best to happen	
I know the value of doing what I love	
I trust my ability to create good things	
My Score	

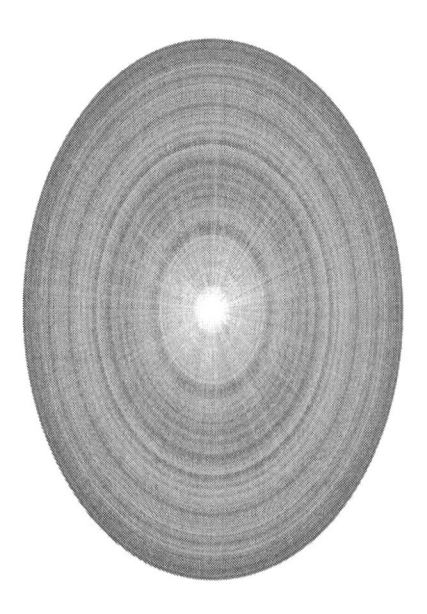

Orange as a Life Purpose Strength: Collaboration & Connection

Orange is a life purpose strength to those of you who are here to bring people together and create unity. With orange as a life purpose strength, you have an ability to bring forth new ideas and involve others in solving problems to make progress towards a common goal.

Collaboration

Those of you with orange as a life purpose strength are born with an understanding of the value of many minds coming together to create meaningful outcomes. Oranges nurture a welcoming space in the world, where people are encouraged to share because they feel safe. Oranges always treat others equally and fairly and encourage collaboration with others with a genuine interest and openness.

Oranges are creative problem solvers as you get others to come together and share skills. Collaboration is a highly evolved skill that enhances relationships and creates good feelings about yourselves and your relationships with others

Connection

Those of you with an orange strength form natural connections with others and seek to bring people together in positive ways. Oranges enjoy creating connections and meaningful relationships with others and need to find your people. You seek connection by joining existing communities or creating your own. Oranges offer security to others through emotional connections that are built on trust and intimacy. Oranges are gifted with the ability to remain unattached to outcomes or agendas, so you create freedom for growth and alignment through your connection to situations in life.

Signs you may have orange as a life purpose strength:
People tell you that you make them feel involved.
You look to work with others to find positive solutions.
You ask other people for their thoughts and ideas.
You love connecting people for their mutual enhancement

Benefits of having an orange strength:
Rich relationships
Emotional intelligence
Trust and emotional security

Top 10 orange life purpose strengths:
Collaboration
Connection
Unification
Solidarity
Togetherness
Family
Warmth
Inclusion
Sharing
Symbiosis

Find out if you have an Orange Life Purpose Strength:

Below, rate yourself on a scale from 1—10 on how accurate the statements are—1 means "not accurate at all," and 10 means "most accurate."

Orange Life Purpose Strength Assessment	Self-Rating
I believe in creating community	
I value the power of people coming together	
I love to involve others in projects	
I love to introduce good people to good people	
I think in terms of teamwork	
I love to make people feel welcome	
I enjoy belonging to groups	
I believe that a rising tide lifts all boats	
I am warm and friendly to others	
I am genuinely interested in others	
My Score	

Red as a Life Purpose Strength: Motivation & Action

Red is a life purpose strength to those of you who are passionate about what you believe in, and you are born motivators. To have red as a life purpose strength means you are here to live a life full of productivity and purposeful action.

Passion

Those of you with red as a life purpose strength are self-propelled action takers who move forwards to accomplish meaningful goals in life. Reds direct your energy towards the things you care about and discover what really matters. Reds understand the value of pursuing passions in order to reveal true callings in life. Doing what you love, doing the things you are drawn to, develops your strengths and natural abilities. Reds' passion for life is optimistic and this optimism is a constant energy booster. The optimism of reds has huge benefits for your overall health and wellbeing. Those of you with red as a strength bring a wonderfully warming and encouraging influence to the world and create a desire in us all to move forwards positively in life.

Motivation

Those of you with red as a strength are natural motivators. Reds generate powerful motivational energy that inspires productivity and action. Reds are highly productive in your lives and with a clear focus you see swift and smooth results. Reds ignite skills in others, live your own dreams, make visions a reality, and aspire to reach your highest potential. Those of you with red as a life purpose strength are generous with your energy and enthusiasm. You produce motivational energy for yourselves and for others, too. Inspirational and motivational energy flows easily from reds and into the lives of others and leaves others feeling empowered and capable. Red strengths bring optimism and a feeling that anything is possible, which increases confidence in the way forwards.

Signs you have a red life purpose strength:
People tell you that you make them feel capable and energized.
You seek out activities that release pent up energy.
You enjoy focussing on getting things done in life.
You are motivated by having goals.

Benefits of having a red strength:

Passion and enthusiasm

Finisher and completer

Highly productive

Top 10 red life purpose strengths:

Passion

Motivation

Purpose

Energy

Action

Productivity

Movement

Personal Power

Potential

Progress

Find Out if You Have a Red Life Purpose Strength:

Below, rate yourself on a scale from 1—10 on how accurate the statements are—1 means "not accurate at all," and 10 means "most accurate."

Red Life Purpose Strength Assessment	Self-Rating
I love to be active	
I have true passions in my life	
I am enthusiastic	
I love meeting new people	
I love the feeling of making progress in life	
It is important for me to be productive	
I love to motivate others	
I am optimistic	
I love to feel motivated	
It is important to be purposeful in my life	
My Score	

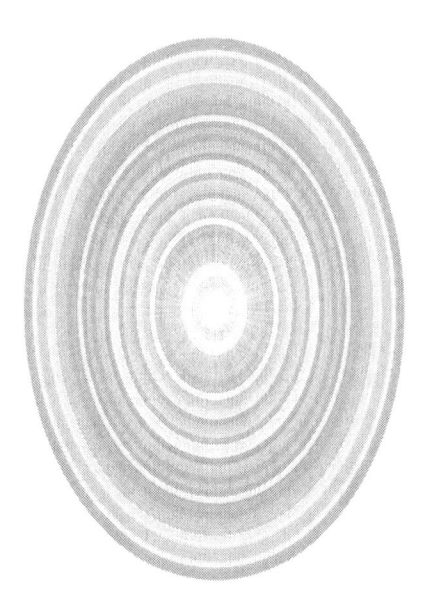

Silver as a Life Purpose Strength: Intuition & Spiritual Growth

Silver is a life purpose strength to those of you who are highly intuitive. With silver as a life purpose strength you understand that your mind, thoughts, and feelings are all powerful tools for imagining and then creating your reality as they want it to be.

Intuition

Those of you with silver as a life purpose strength possess an incredible super power — intuition. Silvers have the ability to know or sense something without reasoning or logic. Increasingly, intuition is credited as being a trusted navigation tool used by many who are successful in life and business. Silvers develop and strengthen your intuition by creating a quiet and peaceful mind. You learn to trust your sense of things and to trust your ability to make good choices about the things that matter to you in life. Silvers develop your intuition by listening to and acting upon your gentle inner voice and have the power to improve all areas of life for the better.

Spiritual Growth

Silvers have remarkable potential for spiritual growth and have the ability to understand the workings of the unseen laws that create our reality. Spirituality is non-denominational and is the energy of interconnectedness between all people, things, thoughts, feelings, and actions. Silvers understand the oneness that we are all intertwined and any change in one affects everything and everyone else. Silvers understand how your thoughts and feelings impact the lives of others around you. You are kind and compassionate people and you fill the world with light and grace.

Signs you may have a silver life purpose strength:
People tell you that you have a positive energy.
You enjoy reading spiritual books and look for alternative solutions.
You see reality differently than others do.
You trust the benevolence of the Universe and know you can create any reality.

Benefits of having a silver strength:
You often *just know* how things will be.
You can plainly see what is unclear to others.
You feel empowered and uplifted by spiritual growth.

Top 10 silver life purpose strengths:

Intuition

Spirituality

Alignment

Ideas

Purifying

Abundance

Femininity

Clarity

Awareness

Focus

Find Out if You Have a Silver Life Purpose Strength:

Below, rate yourself on a scale from 1—10 on how accurate the statements are—1 means "not accurate at all," and 10 means "most accurate."

Silver Life Purpose Strength Assessment	Self-Rating
I believe we are all interconnected	
I love to read books about spirituality	
I believe that I create my own reality	
I want to develop my intuition	
I trust my instincts	
I know my intuition can guide me	
I feel that there is more to me than I currently realise	
I feel drawn to understand how the universe works	
I love seeing signs and symbols to encourage me in my life	
I feel that I am awakening to understand a beautiful new reality	
My Score	

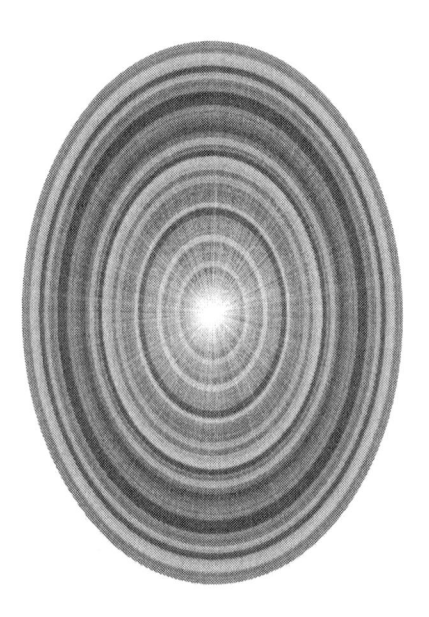

Purple Life Purpose Strength: Change & Forgiveness

Purple, as a life purpose strength, is often present to those of you who are born into a life full of changes and adventures. To have purple as a strength means you are here to create positive outcomes and freeing growth.

Change

Those of you with purple as a life purpose strength are born with the power to create positive change in your own lives and the lives of others. Purples are adaptable and flexible people who embrace change and allow thriving and growth in new circumstances. Purples approach change from the heart and take responsibility for your own peace by understanding the power of your perspective. Purples expect change to lead you to better things and you go inside to find the true source of grounded joy. You show others how to embrace change by freeing yourselves from attachments and, instead, opening your hearts to connect to your highest good.

Forgiveness

Forgiveness is a practice that must begin with yourselves. Those of you with purple as a life purpose strength understand the freedom of healing the wounded parts of yourselves that simply want to be loved. Purples learn that self acceptance brings love to the wounds of your heart and opens your hearts to more love. Love heals all wounds. Purples are loving and tolerant of others to the degree you have learned to refrain from judging and criticising themselves. Purples are liberated through your ability to forgive yourselves and release the guilt, shame, and fear of the past. Each time forgiveness is practised, more space is made for more love and compassion to enter your relationship with yourself and with others. Forgiveness helps you release the fear and regret from your past, so you can transform your present and align yourselves with a future full of love and light. Self-forgiveness begins when you accept that growth is nurtured through love.

Signs you may have a purple life purpose strength:
People tell you they love your calm energy.
You have often felt different from other people.
You find it easy to let go of the past.
You move on quickly from things that weren't meant to be.

Benefits of having a purple life purpose strength:
Very few first-day nerves
Settle in to new roles quickly
You have a live-and-let-live attitude

Top 10 purple life purpose themes
Change
Forgiveness
Transformation
Transmutation
Releasing
Connection
Transition
Friendship
Majesty
Freedom

Find Out if You Have a Purple Life Purpose Strength:

Below, rate yourself on a scale from 1—10 on how accurate the statements are—1 means "not accurate at all," and 10 means "most accurate."

Purple Life Purpose Strength Assessment	Self-Rating
I find it easy to forgive myself	
I find it easy to forgive others	
I am tolerant	
I enjoy change	
I have healed from my past	
I am at peace with my past	
I believe that change can bring blessings	
I believe change can nurture positive growth	
I love doing new things	
I am spontaneous	
My Score	

Now add up your scores and your highest three scores reveal what are likely to be your top three life purpose strengths.

Key Chapter Takeaways

- You have unique life purpose strengths that empower you to live the life you came to live.

- Your guardian angel knows all of your unique life purpose strengths and how you can use them to live your true purpose in life.

- With a good understanding of your unique life purpose strengths, you can easily find and follow your life purpose path.

- Your unique life purpose strengths are the things you are good at doing and being.

- To live your true life purpose, you must know your life purpose strengths and use them in your daily life.

Ros Place

Chapter 13

Building Your Relationship with Your Guardian Angel

"Being deeply loved by someone gives you strength, while loving someone deeply gives you courage."
– Lao Tzu

My hope is that this book inspires you to connect with your guardian angel so you can find and follow your life purpose path using the Channel of Clarity method.

However, as with all things, motivation often leads to frustration when you begin a new process or activity. Rock climbing looks so exciting from the armchair but, once you try to scramble up your first boulder, you quickly discover how much you don't know. The same is true with everything I've shared with you here in this book.

You will, regardless of skill level and desire, eventually run into something that halts your progress towards the ultimate goal of living your true purpose as we've discussed here so far.

In this last chapter, I'd love to provide you with some inspiration through some real-life guardian angels. I'd like to share my own life purpose strengths with you through my beloved guardian angel, Tressarn. With the blessing of some of our wonderful clients, I also share with you some of the beautiful channeled guardian angel messages from our Channel of Clarity sessions together.

Let's start with Tressarn.

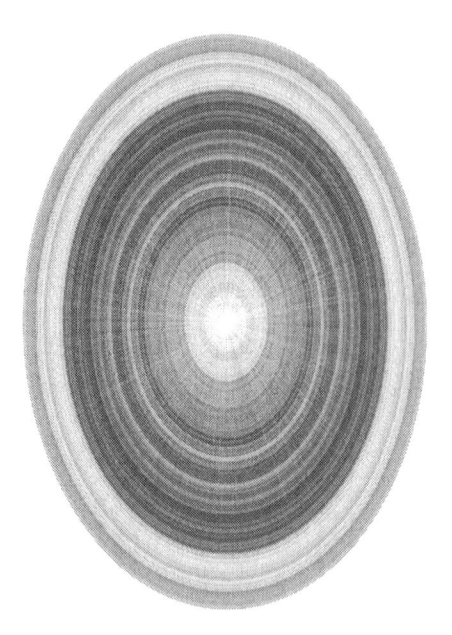

This is Tressarn, my guardian angel — the angel who was assigned to me the moment I was conceived, just as yours was to you. He is with me throughout this whole lifetime and is always by my side, just as yours is by yours. Tressarn is a male energy angel with five bands and his name means Inspirational Encourager. Tressarn's message to me has been to ensure that I prioritise my health in order to succeed in life. This was a much needed lesson for me. For many years, I neglected my health and well-being by pushing myself to the limits of my body's capabilities. I felt, then, that my physical body was an inconvenience and I refused to accept that food, rest, and sleep were necessary in order to thrive. I am pleased to say that I now prioritise my wellbeing and health and that through this, I am enjoying a successful life in all the ways that truly matter to me.

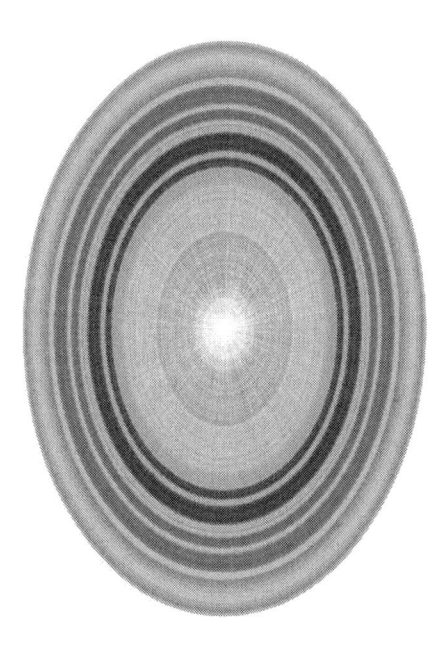

With kind permission from my husband, Eddie, let's meet Prega.

Prega is Eddie's guardian angel. I first met Prega in 2007, when our elder son was very young. I can remember the moment I connected with her. I was deeply moved by her immediate offering of love and nurture. Prega is a female energy angel with six bands and her name means Appreciated Wisdom. Prega's name is significant because in our home we called Eddie, The Bringer of Information! Eddie loves to research and explore subjects and the knowledge he brings into our lives is extremely valuable to us all. Eddie just *knows* good stuff and he knows where to *find* good stuff, too! Prega's message to Eddie is to allow creative expression into his life so that he can succeed in becoming his true and abundant self. This is beyond visible in his life. Eddie enjoys a multitude of outlets for his creativity, from being an excellent baker, to making our soap, producing my skin cream, to writing computer code, and enjoying the interpretations of astrological charts.

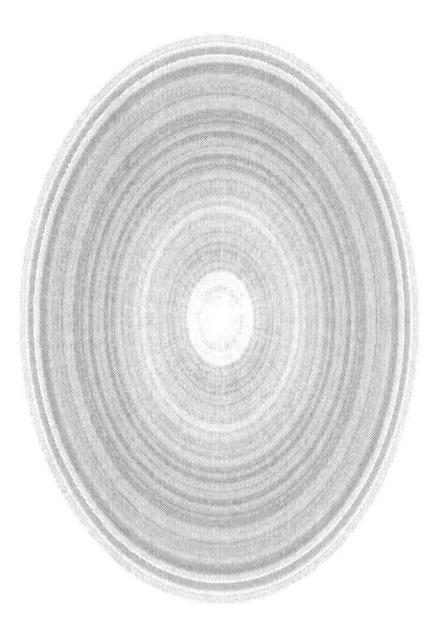

Allow me to introduce Revelatia to you. Revelatia was asked, " How can I maintain the flow (of love)?"

This is my client's channeled reply:

> I love you as I find you each time we connect, each time we enjoy time together. I love the experience of energies coming together. There is a growing fear inside of you that somehow our relationship and connection will not be at its fullest potential in some way when we connect. There is a feeling of managing expectations, the fear of disappointment, as you reach the furthest extremities of opening your heart and allowing the connection, which is so full of love. There is a subtle sense of something disappointing occurring, when expectations have been unmet, left on the table. The experience of disappointment, the pain in your heart is something that you fear returning to.
>
> How can I maintain the flow? It's allowing me to love you as I find you. Knowing that you are lovable in every way. Knowing that the most beautiful relationship that we are creating and enjoying together is one of flow. Flow, by its pure definition, is a process, it is an experience of fluctuation of wonderful peaks, of highest highs, higher than you've ever experienced before, and the flow, which can be experienced as less than that feeling – by comparison – but still a wonderful evolution and development of our relationship and connection, trusting yourself to not be perfect, to not have to arrive perfectly put together, to not have to connect with me when you feel perfect, when your energy is high, when all is well.
>
> Soften your feelings around this. The time when you feel less perfect, simply connect with me to be with me. Think of this more in these times of choosing to spend time together.

Our connection is growing and developing and expanding in magnificent ways. It is an experience of living life at its fullest. Enjoy the experience of being together, spending time and know that however you connect with me, whenever you connect with me, my love is unconditional and your growth continues in love.

And so it is.

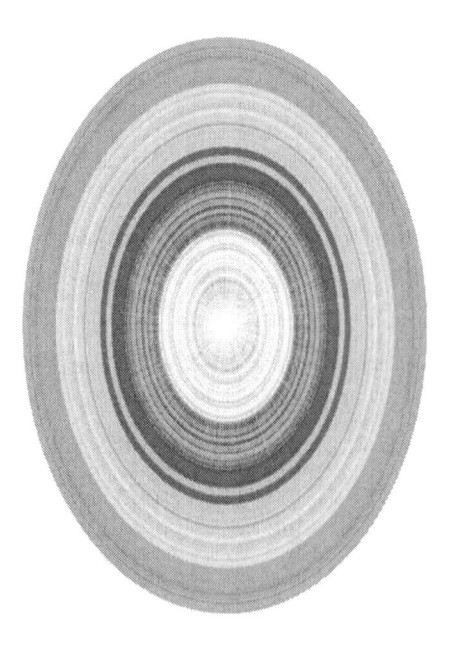

It is my pleasure to introduce you to Emerio.

Emerio was asked " How can I have more lightness of touch (in my life)? "

This is my client's channeled reply:

> It's wonderful that you are reaching a point where you can reach out to me for reassurance. So often, questions are created by you from a place of needing information, requiring data, providing you with information that can be practically applied, a space which needs to be organized or filled, completed, rethought of in some way. And, the most beautiful and the most progress that you make through this question is to ask for reassurance, to ask me to provide you with more love, to ask me to provide you with more encouragement, more light, more love, more positivity, more connection. You are reaching the furthest extremities of your understanding and ability to connect. You're moving outside of all the experiences that you've ever had. And this new space, which you begin to enter into, is a space that can become full of light. All you need to do is open your heart and I am there.
>
> And so it is.

Tressarn shared "How can I learn the technique of Channel of Clarity?"

> Greetings to you friends and guardian angels. It is wonderful to connect with you. It is wonderful that we come together in this way to communicate and to cocreate in the most joyful of ways to understand new ways of being, which allow us and

empower us to create a truly blissful experience here on earth, and to access realities which may be invisible to so many.

Today, I wish to speak of technique, of a method, a process, a rational thinking pathway, which you are learning as you create your Channel of Clarity. The rational thinking pathway, which you are learning, is important in order that you may embed in your mind a process which can be followed.

The rational thinking mind requires you to learn through practice, through repetition, in order that a process can become automated. The example that I gave to Ros earlier today is that of driving a car. When you drive a car, you learn so much of what is necessary to drive a car and think of all the pieces, the pedals under your feet, the steering, the awareness of other vehicles, looking in mirrors, ensuring that you are safe, that you understand the road layouts. But once we have learned the technique, you then experience driving without thinking. Ros experiences driving without thinking where she can make journeys at times and not remember the journey when she arrives, not fully remember how she got there. The technique has been learned. The body knows the technique. The mind is no longer required. It can function happily being occupied by a task, being occupied by a technique, which then frees you, provides space in you in order to access another way of being, an automatic mode. Through the automatic mode, a quietness, a peace, a silent stillness opens and a knowing can be experienced, which can't be described by language or words but can be felt, felt and sensed and absorbed and radiated within. It's an experience of resonance.

When you learn technique, when you consistently practice technique, when you apply yourself to a task, to the point at which it becomes automatic, and within a task, which you know is achievable, you open up a part of yourself in which there is space. Ros tells me that there were times when she felt that she would never understand how to drive a car. In fact, it was important for her to be tested twice to learn how to drive her car. But, she never disbelieved that it was possible because there were so many others driving their cars. There was evidence everywhere of others who had learned the technique and who drove their cars. There was no doubt that driving her car was possible. And so it is the same with learning this technique of channeling your guardian angel. The technique is being learned.

Its practice becomes a space from which you are able to access an essence, a resonance of feeling, a sense, and it is from this place that your channel of connection will become amplified. It is reality that your channel is created between you and your guardian angel, and that it already exists. It is you escaping from the mind. It is your ability to give yourself to the technique in such a way as you are able to bridge the gap between knowledge and knowing. And, it is only familiarity of the technique that will provide you with that experience. There is so much love for you. I am so full of love for you and your angels. You are on a path of true magnificence. There is so much love now. There is so much love that lies ahead.

And so it is.

Tressarn was asked "How will I know it is my guardian angel?"

How will I know it is my guardian angel? How will I know it is their voice, their presence and not another angel or higher guide? Each guardian angel has a sound, a tone, a resonance, which is individual and unique to that guardian angel, to your guardian angel. And, the way you will begin to develop familiarity with that tone, of the beautiful resonance of that note or sound, is from the feeling of love, of I love you. When you place your hand on your heart and say 'I love you,' the resonance, the sound and the feeling of I love you, creates a space for you to feel the tone which is their signature.

And so it is.

Pretty incredible guardian angel messages, right?

Connecting with guardian angels for my clients is really, really enjoyable. It's always so awe inspiring for clients to see their guardian angels and receive their messages for the very first time.

Why am I telling you all this?

Because I want you to know that **you have a guardian angel just as beautiful, just as ready to guide you to live your true purpose path, as all the women you've read about in this book.**

You have unique strengths and a valuable contribution that the world needs you to make in this lifetime. You have a unique life purpose and a guardian angel waiting to guide you so you can live your highest good. You can change your own life for the better and the lives of your loved ones. Do it a little at a time or all at once. What matters is that you do everything you can to live your true purpose in life and just to get doing so as soon as you can.

So, before moving on in this book, make a choice.

How are you going to

> A. get your guardian angel's name and connection established so you know all your unique strengths and life purpose path?
>
> B. get your Channel of Clarity ready so you have two-way communication with your guardian angel and you can receive all the life purpose guidance you will ever need?

If you tell yourself that you'll *figure it out later,* you may never get to it. It'll just be another idea heaped on top of all the others that got sorted into the figure-it-out-later category. Make a choice now, whatever it might be, and commit to getting started. The world needs you, now more than ever, so step up and get out there and live your true purpose in life.

Key Chapter Takeaways

- When it comes to the strategies we've talked about in this book, committing to these two areas will get you started:
  1. Connecting with your guardian angel
     - His or her name
     - His or her colours
     - His or her number
     - Your unique life purpose strengths
  2. The channel of clarity to receive answers and life purpose guidance
     - Good questions
     - Clear answers
     - Clear guidance for every step of the way
     - Flowing two-way communication so you can live your true life purpose

Ros Place

Conclusion

Starting Your Life Purpose Journey

What to Do Next?

We've reached the end of our time together, my friend. I sincerely hope that you've benefited in many ways from what you have read.

To recap what we've covered:

1. In the first few chapters of this book, we took a deep look at the status of your life today.

    We looked at how much of your life was in line with your true life purpose, what areas needed improving, and even prescribed a few courses of action based on the results of your assessments.

    You should have a clear picture in your mind of where you can improve quickly and how **Channel of Clarity** might be the key to solving your challenges.

2. Next, we looked at all the ways that your guardian angel—the key to your life purpose—could reveal your life purpose path and guide you to live your true purpose in life.

3. We also took a look at the challenges and hurdles that come with connecting with your guardian angel and how you know you have established your connection.

4. In the next big chapter of the book, we explored creating your **Channel of Clarity,** for crystal clear, two-way direct communication with your guardian angel.

    We took a look at the **The Celestial Formula** for guaranteeing your ability to live your true life purpose with your guardian angel. We examined each of the three stages required for success, and we also spent time looking at how you can receive real-time guidance about every question you could ever wish to ask.

    By the end, we explored all the unique aspects of the method and how to connect the dots, so you can receive all the guidance you need to live your true life purpose, easily.

5. Then, we focused on creating your Channel of Clarity, your direct communication line to your guardian angel, in four steps: Heart Centre State, Calling in your Guardian Angel's Light, Becoming Charged with Your Guardian Angel's Light, and Creating Your Channel of Clarity, with a walkthrough for you to follow.

    You should have a strong understanding of what you need to do next to get started creating your Channel of Clarity and receiving guidance that will change your life forever.

6. Last of all, we returned to how to discover your unique life purpose strengths.

    We looked at the Nine Core Life Purpose Strengths and you identified your likely top three strengths to guarantee you know your true purpose in life.

We also spent time exploring my and others' guardian angels, their names, numbers and even some channeled messages from real-life guardian angels.

Finally, we looked at realistic plans for implementing this method, getting your connection with your guardian angel in place, and ensuring your success as you pursue this highly effective life purpose discovery method.

What is next can be said in a word:

Begin

Make one small choice. Take one small step. Channel your guardian angel and live your true glorious life purpose.

You'll be forever grateful you did.

With love to you and your guardian angel,

Ros & Tressarn xx

Book Bonuses

If you are like me, when you start a project, you want to know as much as you can about what you are studying. In the spirit of gratitude and in my desire to give you more information that fits between the covers of this book, here are some resources with the information you seek.

Over the Shoulder — Guardian Angel Walkthrough with Tressarn, Ros's Guardian Angel

In this video training, I'll walk you through Tressarn's and Prega's colours and life purpose strengths to help you to understand your own. Knowing your life purpose strengths and how to apply them to your life is the most important part of living your true purpose with your guardian angel. In this training, you'll learn about my guardian angel in ways that will help you to understand your own.

channelofclarity.com/book-bonus

Your Life Purpose Strength Areas — A Deeper Dive

One of the most-loved aspects of coaching students is my deeper dive into the areas of life purpose strengths. In this training, you'll explore what those life purpose areas are and how to connect them with your guardian angel's number and your unique life purpose strengths.

channelofclarity.com/book-bonus

Channel of Clarity PDF Book

Enhance your reading experience with the printable PDF version of this book. See all the colours and enjoy all the self-assessments and life purpose discovery exercises inside the PDF version of the book.

channelofclarity.com/book-bonus

Ros Place

We Can Help You Even More

Tressarn and I hope you enjoyed reading The Channel of Clarity Method and your free book bonuses. As a born guardian angel channel I love to help you in any way I can to channel your own guardian angel. Tressarn and I are delighted to share more ways that can help you to channel your guardian angel:

Channel of Clarity 12-Month Personal Program

Our most popular next step to channel your guardian angel is our 12-Month Personal Program. It shows you how to channel your guardian angel in just 30 minutes a day from the comfort of your own home.

Please visit **channelofclarity.com/personal-program**

1:1 Mentoring Program with Ros

If you'd like to know more about how I can personally mentor you to channel your guardian angel, please book a chat here:

Just click **channelofclarity.com/call**

Guardian Angel Readings

I offer a waitlist for personal guardian angel readings, if you would like to join my waitlist you can register here:

Please visit **channelofclarity.com/readings**

Please don't hesitate to reach out to us with any comments or questions at **support@channelofclarity.com**

With love to you and your guardian angel,

Ros & Tressarn xx

Ros Place

About the Author

Ros Place was born channeling angels and her earliest memory is of watching angels around her in her crib. Ros grew up in Kent, in the south of England, in a family of muggles and had to navigate life with the angels without guidance or support from the people in her life. Thanks to Tressarn's constant guidance and infinite love, Ros was able to channel her way out of homelessness and into her true life purpose, a life of impact, and helping others.

When she's not channeling guardian angels, Ros enjoys long walks in the woods, spending time with her husband Eddie and their sons, preparing and eating good food, and testing out new coffee shops.

Above all, Ros believes that family comes first and that living your true life purpose should be a catalyst for improving the lives of those you love most. That includes living an abundant life that provides time, peace, freedom, and joy.

All inquiries for podcast appearances, video shows, and speaking can be sent to support@channelofclarity.com

Channel of Clarity Method

Ros Place

Printed in Great Britain
by Amazon